LOST
ABERDEEN

*

IN MEMORIAM

Ian B.D. Bryce FSA Scot
1935–2001

Cuthbert Graham LLD
1911–1987

LOST
ABERDEEN

ABERDEEN'S LOST
ARCHITECTURAL HERITAGE

Diane Morgan

BIRLINN

BY THE SAME AUTHOR

In the Villages of Aberdeen series
Footdee
Round About Mounthooly
The Spital
The Spital Lands
Old Aberdeen Volume 1
Lost Aberdeen. The Outskirts

A Monumental Business:
The Story of A & J Robertson (Granite) Ltd
1876–2001

First published in 2004 by
Birlinn Limited
West Newington House
10 Newington Road
Edinburgh EH9 1QS

Reprinted with corrections, 2007

www.birlinn.co.uk

ISBN13: 978 1 84158 390 7
ISBN10: 1 84158 390 1

British Library Cataloguing-in-Publication Data
A catalogue record for this book is available
from the British Library.

Design: Mark Blackadder

Printed and bound by
The Cromwell Press, Trowbridge, Wiltshire

CONTENTS

INTRODUCTION AND ACKNOWLEDGEMENTS

The ancient buildings of Aberdeen are, like those of most of our Scottish towns, rapidly disappearing ... Perth which was famous for its churches and houses has been swept bare; hardly anything remains in Dumfries or Ayr; and Glasgow which half a century ago was rich in ancient remains, has lost nearly everything, including its splendid college. Since the few following sketches of Aberdeen buildings were made, the most picturesque of them all – the old house on the School Hill – has been taken down ...

The 'old house on the School Hill' was the artist George Jamesone's turreted mansion, demolished in 1886 to create additional stabling for the carters, Wordie & Co Ltd.

Thus the architects David MacGibbon and Thomas Ross bemoaned Scotland's regrettable demolitions in their monumental illustrated account of *The Castellated and Domestic Architecture of Scotland from the Twelfth to the Eighteenth Century*. For the Aberdeen section in Volume 5, published in 1892, MacGibbon and Ross had also sketched 'the Bishop's Palace' i.e. Mar's Castle of 1595 in the Gallowgate (they were occasionally vague about names), removed in 1897 to 'improve the amenity', the seventeenth century turreted house next to Lord Byron's in Broad Street, which was demolished along with its neighbours in 1902 to make way for the new Marischal College façade, and the Wallace Tower (Benholm's Lodging) of 1593, taken down in 1963 to give Marks & Spencer a better site, and ignominiously carted off to Tillydrone in the back of a lorry.

While much demolition between the 1880s and the 1930s was, as one would expect, carried out in the name of slum clearance, some was for road widening, and some, as early as 1886, as we have seen, was to further commercial development. An older philosophy of, 'it's aul', ding it doon', also existed. The great architect Archibald Simpson (1790–1847) was no conservationist, impatient to get rid of the old, however architecturally interesting, if it was in his way, in favour of the new. How fortunate that he and his colleague, that other creator of the granite city, the city architect John Smith (1781–1852), worked in a graceful, neo-classical idiom. Around 1900 the Aberdeen master mason John Morgan wrote: 'We have public parks and open spaces, palatial schools and finer churches, but all this is poor compensation for a good deal of ruthless and wholesale destruction of many old and time-honoured landmarks that can never be brought back. Perhaps Morgan was weeping crocodile tears as he demolished the fine old House of Rubislaw to replace it in 1887 with his, admittedly, unique and splendid mansion, now No. 50 Queen's Road. But in the 1880s, there were still vacant feus in the developing west-end of Aberdeen where Morgan, with his insider knowledge about the availability of land, could have located his art nouveau masterpiece without a guilty conscience.

And so on it went. The Aberdeen architect, artist and historian, Fenton Wyness, who died in 1974, a man before his time in the field of conservation, must have noted with regret that his role in turning back the tide of demolition in Aberdeen was as successful as King Canute's activities on the sea shore. He wrote bitterly in *City By the Grey North Sea: Aberdeen* (1965); 'Nothing of the burgh's vast architectural heritage remains in Exchequer Row, the Green, the Netherkirkgate, Schoolhill, Broad Street and the Gallowgate, once one of the finest streets in Scotland'. The Gallowgate, where there existed such a strong sense of community, suffered almost a century of piecemeal demolition which began with Mar's Castle in 1897 and continued until 1986 when the listed buildings between St Paul Street and the former premises of Ogston & Tennant, soap manufacturers, were removed to make way for the Bon Accord Centre and its adjuncts. Over the years the Gallowgate's north end had been filled with a scattering of ugly low and high rise flats and the grim Aberdeen College, a landscape well described as 'a jumble of unrelated rubbish'.

In *Aberdeen, Century of Change* (1971) Fenton Wyness summed up:

> The changes which have taken place are almost beyond belief. The demolition of the Guestrow and Gallowgate – enacted under heading of slum clearance – was a major disaster. True, the properties there had been allowed to develop into slums – but the architectural and historic value of the majority of the houses far outweighed the unsanitary conditions that eventually sealed their doom. The condition of the Guestrow and Gallowgate properties was no worse – and in some case better – than those now restored

in Edinburgh's Royal Mile, in Old Aberdeen's High Street and Don Street ... This unique area which had it been preserved as a whole, might well have become the city's greatest tourist attraction.

The war brought a temporary halt to demolition in Aberdeen, at least by those on the allied side, but with the peace, battle stations were taken up again. The new ethos of conservation was seen as a west-end preserve, not on the agenda of those councillors who were more intent on building council houses in every ward than saving the city's heritage. The importance of Union Street and the Granite City to Scottish architecture was not appreciated by all, and that old mantra, 'it's aul', ding it doon' was still being chanted. However there were cross-party alliances in the city among those who argued successfully for the preservation of Provost Ross's House of 1593, and Sir George Skene's Mansion (Provost Skene's House), from 1545, both of which had earlier been given their marching orders. The restorations were excellent and most Aberdonians were pleasantly surprised. In 1971 virtually the whole city was united against the destruction of the New Market, unfortunately to no avail.

Pre-war demolitions had been largely a case of 'wer ain sea guts to wer ain sea maws', but the big time developer appeared in Aberdeen after hostilities ceased, and the focus was on Union Street and commercial gain, presented as city centre improvements. Some in key positions were flattered that developers south of the city were taking an interest in Aberdeen. 'Listed building consent' was slickly operated, though fortunately not always acted on. There were architectural 'turkeys' below the standard of what was acceptable in Union Street, the 'broiler house' block between Huntly Street and the Music Hall, the fenestration of BhS, which must be the ugliest in Scotland. At the same time, well-loved shops whose frontages harmonised with the street, were forced out, a result of factors such as rising business rates and the advent of the supermarket. There are only three locally owned shops in Union Street in 2007. Though this once great street is the city's prime conservation area, its visual aspect, once a breathtaking panorama, has deteriorated over the past half century. A fair number of its elegant, listed buildings, though not physically lost, have fallen from architectural grace, raped by vast plate glass windows for which they were never designed, demeaned by tawdry frontages and the garish trappings of corporate identity. The power to redeem Union Street lies with the local authority, but heavy-handed enforcement may not be necessary. In some cases the application of soap and water, and a mandatory painting scheme would bring about considerable improvement.

While Union Street was declining, plans were afoot for the total demolition of St Nicholas Street and part of George Street and its environs, a great chunk of the city's small central townscape. The St Nicholas Street/George Street area, a vibrant, cheerful place with a wide range of price-conscious shops, was the housewife's favourite shopping area, more so than Union Street. In 1964 Aberdeen City Council designated it a Central Comprehensive Development Area. Some dereliction had been identified and the only solution the council would entertain was wholesale destruction and redevelopment, a course of action once popular in Europe and the UK, but beginning to go out of fashion. To those who shopped there, this seemed an extraordinarily draconian course of action.

A spirited, well-informed George Street Traders' group was formed which opposed the council's 'clean sweep' approach. It promoted a new strategy which was beginning to be adopted elsewhere, gradual redevelopment rather than total upheaval, demolition where necessary, and upgrading of the better properties, of which there were many in the area. All the ingredients for an ideal 'makeover' were present; the restoration of the intriguing pends and closes in the Upperkirkgate and Schoolhill; Donald's Court to the west and Drum's Lane to the east, linking up and leading into attractively designed courtyards; a well-placed shopping mall and discreet multi-storey parking; St Nicholas Street, the ideal pedestrian precinct. If only the neighbouring Guestrow and the Wallace Tower – what other city had a Z-plan towerhouse in its centre? – had survived, been restored and incorporated in such a scheme, Aberdeen could have had one of the most attractive, indigenous and unique city centres in Scotland, as financially valuable to the city as the 1960s-style shopping centres that were envisaged.

The traders' plans were dismissed. Discussions between the aspiring developers and property owners and retailers about ways of improving the area other than by wholesale demolition were not an option. Planning blight set in, residents endured years of stress and uncertainty and eventually had no choice but to sell out. In spite of sustained opposition, by far the greater part of the 'clean sweep' project survived and in the fullness of time two covered malls emerged from a landscape that had long resembled the Somme. The St Nicholas Centre was opened in 1985, the Bon Accord Centre in 1990, tenanted by the usual multiples.

Two unfortunate consequences should have been foreseen. Firstly, instead of utilising 'dead' land between streets as, for example, the modern Trinity Centre and the Academy do, and as the old New Market and Co-op Arcade used to, the St Nicholas Centre annihilated St Nicholas Street, while the Bon Accord Centre straddled George Street, blocking off its northern end, rendering it a virtual lost place. Secondly, an exodus of middle range shops to the Bon Accord Centre made it difficult to lure quality retailers to fill the now empty shops in Union Street, whose problems have been exacerbated in recent years by a burgeoning drinks' culture. Through too few interesting shops and too many pubs and drinking halls, it is lost to many Aberdonians. One of the saddest sights in the evening is the white shirts of the admission consultants glowing in the dusk as their wearers stand guard outside the numerous licensed premises in the street's west end.

In the latter half of the twentieth century much that used to be synonymous with Aberdeen has been lost. Rubislaw Quarry has closed down, the granite and trawling industries, the Gordon Highlanders, Hall Russells' and John Lewis's Shipyards, J & J Crombie at Grandholm Mills and Richards at Broadford have all gone. The names of the Dons are no longer household ones. There is no Co-op Arcade, no New Market, no Watt & Grant, no Rubber Shop, no Woodside Fountain, no students at Marischal College and no Students' Union. In the Upperkirkgate no High School for Girls, no GPO in Crown Street, no St Nicholas Street, no south end of George Street and consequently no view across to Torry. Collies and the aroma of roasting coffee beans is gone forever. In a city desperately short of art galleries and museums in which to display its collections, James Dun's House, which staged many small local exhibitions, has been sold off and is now a beauty parlour. Grampian Television has been acquired by Scottish Television with the Queen's Cross studios, a former tram depot, replaced by flats. Beechgrove House has gone and the BBC work out of modest accommodation nearby. The Kirk o Nigg, the Denburn Kirk, Holburn Central and Greyfriars Kirk, all once prominent parish churches, have closed their doors. Losses since 2003 include, in Union Street, the well-known, long-established department store, Esslemont & Macintosh, at Nos 26–38 which closed in May 2007; the conversion of Bakers' wonderful china shop at No 136, on the original ground floor of Archibald Simpson's Aberdeen Hotel, (1826–7) into a DVD store; while the restrained, elegant No. 122, built in 1836–7 for James Allan, cabinetmaker, more recently occupied by Mothercare, is to become an amusement arcade. Here the Scottish Executive upheld an appeal by the developers against Aberdeen City Council. What sort of signal does that put out?

Lost Aberdeen attempts to record at least some part of the city's vanished architectural heritage, and the sense of personal loss that has gone with it. Part One deals with the old burgh with its ports, (gates), gates, (roads), rows, (terraces), pends, (arched entrances) and closes, (courts); the second part, with the post-1800 new town. Vanished buildings and long gone streets, have filled the book to overflowing. A final chapter examines Old Aberdeen where, conversely, buildings tended to be utterly ruinous before they were taken down and even then their stones were sold on. Much more remains to be examined.

Many people have advised in a number of ways during the writing of *Lost Aberdeen*. I owe a debt of gratitude to Grant Simpson, Bruce and Midge Miller, Frank Donnelly, Norman Marr, Catherine Taylor, Mike Dey, Alison Cameron, Steven McRae, and to MacAberdeen for technical assistance. Pat Sutherland has given splendid support and my husband, David I. Morgan has patiently assisted in my search for traces of vanished buildings. Keith Jones and Jimmy Brown commented knowledgeably on the Schoolhill Station; Paul Pillath (who also kindly assisted with illustrations), Connie Leith and the staff of Funeralcare helped trace the whereabouts of the Northern Co-op Memorial. Tom and Bill Cramond gave invaluable details of the Wallace Tower pub as student houff. Sadly neither has lived to see his memories in print. I was privileged to have access to research carried out by John Souter and George Gordon over many years while Robert Gibb and Alex Guyan kindly placed their photographic collections at my disposal; Winram's Bookshop assisted with illustrative material as did Ian Olson, Martin Watt, Lottie Booth and James Kellas. The photo of La Scala is from the *Bon Accord* per Michael Thomson's seminal work, *Silver Screen in the Silver City*, 1988. J. A. Sutherland provided charming illustrations as well plans of Huxter Row and the Wallace Tower area. Last but not least, a posthumous thanks to James Gordon, Parson of Rothiemay (1615–1686), the greatest cartographer of them all.

I have pleasure in acknowledging permission to reproduce copyright photographs provided by the following sources and individuals:

Aberdeen Art Gallery & Museums Collections, pages 106, 118
Aberdeen City Council, pages 29, 42, 207 (bottom), 210 (bottom)
Aberdeen Library and Information Services, pages 15, 105, 108,
     109, 110, 112, 167, 168, 187, 194
Robert Gibb, pages 97 (bottom), 147, 184, 204, 213
Alex Guyan, pages 98, 140, 167 (left, top right), 206, 212
RCAHMS pages 67, 128, with thanks to Lynn Earley

DIANE MORGAN, 2004

PART 1
Royal Burgh

*

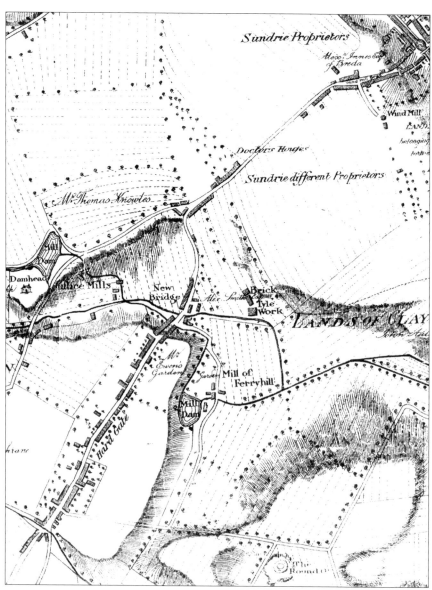

The road to Aberdeen straggled north-east from the Bridge of Dee, through the Hardgate with its complex road junction, bottom left, passed above the Ferryhill Mill Dam, over the New Bridge, centre, (the junction of the Hardgate and Union Glen today), eventually to descend to the hamlet of Windmill Brae, top right, and over the tiny Bow Brig to the Green. Detail from Capt George Taylor's Plan of Aberdeen, 1773.

CHAPTER 1

THE ROAD
TO ABERDEEN

FROM THE HARDGATE
TO THE CASTLEGATE

*

THE HARDGATE

Lord Medwyn, a judge who came to Aberdeen on circuit both before and after the building of Union Street, once uttered a memorable aphorism, the first half of which was that Aberdeen was a city without an entrance. This was more or less true. Before 1805 and for several years after, the traveller from the south, having crossed the River Dee, had to find his way to the

The Hardgate in 1887. It was for many years a village in its own right.
From the watercolour by I. W. Davidson.

Bridge of Dee Road and pass through the now long-vanished lands of Tillyneedly, Pitmuxton and Cuparstone. After a mile and a half or so, the Bridge of Dee Road merged into the Hardgate, a 'hard' or made-up road (gate being Scots for road), as opposed to the usual muddy footpath. This was a major crossroads where the present-day Holburn, Broomhill and Fonthill Roads and the Bridge of Dee Road/Hardgate all came together. Here there was a settlement which took the name of the road it flanked, the Hardgate, which could have been mistaken for the entrance to Aberdeen.

THE HOUSE OF BETHANY

✳

By the late eighteenth century the Hardgate boasted a scattering of fine villas, Elmbank, Millbank, Rosebank and Willowbank, so named because their gardens sloped down to the embankment that retained the Ferryhill Mill dam. Prominent among these was Bellevue, the pocket estate of the brewer William Black, 'with its thriving plantings and well of good water'. It was put up for sale in 1828 as 'a most desirable and elegant residence such as is seldom on the market'. A later owner, Mrs Elizabeth White of Perth, had founded an order of Episcopalian sisters, the Scottish Society of Reparation, later the Society of St Mary and St John, in memory of her late husband. The

The House and Chapel of Bethany, Hardgate, Aberdeen.

Old buildings in the Hardgate, centre and left. None survive.
The pend, right, now gives access to 'Bethany Gardens'.

order was devoted to the care of orphans and she had come to Aberdeen on the invitation of local Episcopalians to establish a convent and orphanage. Bellevue, which Mrs White renamed the House of Bethany, had spacious grounds and was ideally situated for the new convent. She enlarged the house, added a chapel of her own design and remained Mother Superior of the order until her death in 1893.

The community continued its work quietly in Ferryhill for the best part of a century, but by 1976, with the orphans gone and only one sister left, the convent closed. Attempts to have the building listed and retained, possibly as student accommodation in an open setting, failed. Developers were waiting in the wings and the House of Bethany and its chapel were demolished. Today modern housing, 'Bethany Gardens', occupies the site.

WINDMILL BRAE

*

Beyond the villas, a muddy, steep brae climbed to a sparsely populated part of the Hardgate, now Langstane Place, then on to Windmill Brae, like the original Hardgate, a settlement in its own right. It took its name from the windmill which stood a little to the south, at the present Crown Terrace. Windmill Brae led down to the Bow Brig then across the Denburn, which flowed from the west through the heart of the city and so to the Green.

Lower Windmill Brae was swept away by the arrival of the Denburn Valley Junction Railway in 1864, linking the north and south railways to Aberdeen with their terminus at the new, aptly named Joint Station at Guild Street. What remains of Windmill Brae is now a dreary 'publand' street, not recommended to the solitary traveller at night.

Lower Windmill Brae. Beyond the houses, the lampposts on the balustrades of the Bow Brig can be made out and beyond that, the seven-storey woollen mill of Alex Hadden & Sons, which straddled, in modern terms, the Green, Guild Street and Rennie's Wynd.

THE BOW BRIG

*

The Bow Brig, spanning the Denburn, marked the western limits of the city and was the nearest thing to an entrance that the town had before Union Street. Travellers to Aberdeen from the south had to cross it, but it was so diminutive they might not have realised its importance until, if they were visitors of distinction, they found themselves welcomed by the magistrates. Several Bow Brigs were built over the years. In 1556 the haill toun (the town council) instructed a substantial two-arched bridge to cope with the

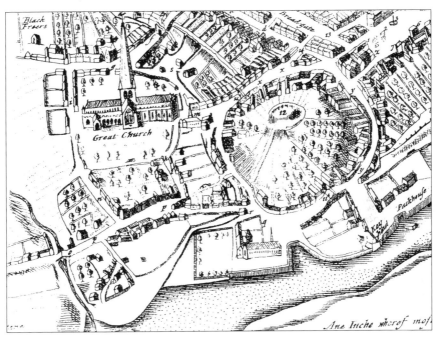

From extreme left, (o) is the Bow Brig with the Denburn flowing below; (p) indicates the Green and the big house between the (p)s is Aedie's Lodging; (q) is the Trinity Friars' Place with the Keyhead or Quay and Packhouse or Weigh-House right. The Shiprow (y) wound round the southern and eastern slopes of St Catherine's Hill, marked (12) which dominated the townscape. It then merged with the Netherkirkgate marked (x) on the northern side of the hill. (Banish Union Street from the mind). The western side, unmarked and going downhill in all senses, was Putachieside. It joined up with the Shiprow near the Trinity Friars' Place, and the roadway around St Catherine's Hill came full circle. Shore Brae is the broad, unmarked road between the Keyhead and Packhouse. The Shiprow Port (11) left of the top of Shore Brae, one of the city's six defensive ports, from the French la porte, gate, dated from the first half of the fifteenth century. (All ports were demolished before the eighteenth century was out as they were impeding the flow of traffic!) Detail from Parson Gordon of Rothiemay's Plan of 1661.

additional traffic into town generated by Bishop Gavin Dunbar's new Bridge of Dee of 1527. In 1609 David Anderson of Finzeauch, 'Davy-do-a'thing', mathematician, engineer and councillor in charge of building work, was instructed to erect a new two-arched bridge. The contractor was his brother-in-law, Andrew Jamesone, master mason and father of the renowned portrait painter, George Jamesone. This was the bridge that Montrose's Royalist forces crossed after the Battle of Justice Mills, in September 1644, bent on sacking Aberdeen. The Brig featured again in the final skirmish between Royalists and Covenanters in May 1646.

Double-arched bridges had been fashionable for a couple of centuries but when the Denburn came down in spate to its estuary at the harbour, the Bow Brig's arches hampered the flow of water, causing the Green to flood, damaging the property of residents. In November 1746 complaints were made

The Bow Brig in the centre middle ground appears to nestle below the mighty span of Union Bridge, a short distance upstream. The houses of Windmill Brae are to the right, those of the Green to the left. Hadden's Mill looms beyond. Extreme right, the trees of the Corby Heugh, the future Union Terrace Gardens. Detail from a sketch by J.W. Allan, 1839.

to the town council about flood damage as well as the dangerous condition of the bridge itself. The magistrates ordered the mason, John Jeans, to replace it with a single-span Bow Brig.

THE PUFFIN' BRIGGIE

*

By 1850 the heavily polluted Denburn was declared a public nuisance and filled in. The Bow Brig straddled dry land for some months, then was taken down and part of it resurrected in an alcove in Union Terrace Gardens, where it languishes in anonymity. When the railway was built in 1865–7, a new bridge, nicknamed the Puffin' Briggie, replaced the Bow Brig. When trains passed underneath, they gave the illusion that the bridge was puffing steam. Boys used to place their caps on the gaps in the decking to see how high the steam would lift them and I remember from childhood that crossing when a steam train was passing underneath was exciting, if terrifying. The

The Puffin' Briggie with Bridge Street beyond.

9

Puffin' Briggie was removed in 1982 when the Trinity Centre was under construction. The right of way to the Green now runs through the middle of a dismal multi-storey carpark.

THE GREEN

The Bow Brig gave access to the west end of the Green, the *vicus viridis* (the green highway), though by Parson Gordon's time and doubtless long before that it was an oddly shaped street without a hint of green. It appears in records from 1273. The Green is a contender for the 'cradle of Aberdeen' title, though the jury is still out on that issue, as it is based on the existence of William the Lion's alleged palace there. Robert the Bruce is said to have stayed in the palace in 1308 after the Battle of Barra. Christian Bruce, Robert's sister, did, however, live in the Green in later life and gifted a silver chalice set with precious stones to the Mither Kirk of St Nicholas. In 1336, during the Second War of Independence, the Green was the scene of a terrible slaughter of townsmen who stood against a professional force of English soldiers led by Sir Thomas Roscelyn. His death in the affray led, on the orders of Edward III, to a reprisal burning of Aberdeen that lasted over six days. There was further turmoil during the Protestant Reformation of 1560 when a Carmelite Monastery, bounded in modern terms by the Green, Rennies Wynd, Martin's Lane and Carmelite Street, was destroyed by the 'rascal multitude' sent north by the Protestant barons of Angus and the Mearns to introduce Aberdonians to the reformed religion.

The Green was chiefly famous for the weekly open-air market of dairy produce which has taken place there since the sixteenth century, when Aberdeen was a thriving burgh of around 7,000. The location was ideal, on the busy route between the Bow Brig and the commercial and social heart of the city at the Castlegate. The Green was handy for the shore, it was sheltered and the great parish kirk of St Nicholas looming above was a deterrent to cheats and shysters.

ÆDIE'S LODGING
*

The Green was built up by the late sixteenth century and the townhouse lodging of the maltsman Andrew Ædie was one of the finest there. It was erected some time before 1604, possibly by the master mason Andrew

Jamesone. It stood not far from the Bow Brig, at the foot of a wynd to which the Ædies gave their name. In these pre-Union Street days one could clamber up this steep brae to reach St Nicholas Kirk, via Westerkirkgate, later Back Wynd. George, one of the later Ædies, married Mary Jamesone, daughter of the painter and granddaughter of the mason. She was a renowned embroiderer and two years after her death in 1684, George Ædie sold her four exquisite needlework panels to the Master of Kirk and Brig Work for £400 Scots. They were later hung at the entrance to the former Kirk of West St Nicholas, where they can still be seen.

Ædie's Lodging was harled, three storeys high, with a steep-pitched, slated roof. The original, tiny garret windows have been replaced by skylights. In 1633 the then owner, David Ædie, who would fall at the Justice Mills, added the dormer windows and embellished their tympana, the triangular window-heads, with his heraldic arms and those of his wife, Kathren Burnet, which bear the horn of the Burnetts of Leys. Such adornment, a proclamation of status, was de rigueur for married couples who built or acquired a house of substance. Ædie's Wynd lies next to the house and the Back Wynd Stairs are just visible in the distance. Built at the same time as Union Street, they replaced the lower half of Back Wynd, and much of Ædie's Wynd.

PETER WILLIAMSON'S PRISON
*

In the 1750s unwary young boys playing near Aberdeen harbour might have found themselves kidnapped, imprisoned in nearby houses till a ship became available, transported to the Americas and sold into the slave trade. This 'detestable trafficking', notorious in Aberdeen, was controlled by the town's officials and magistrates, including Provost More of Raeden. No one had the courage to expose it until one of the kidnapped boys, Peter Williamson, after incredible adventures, returned to Aberdeen and brought his former captors to justice.

The street sign indicates the Back Wynd Stairs and shows the rough cobbles of the lower end of Aedie's Wynd. The houses here fronted the lower end of the Wynd, not the Green. The narrow Forbes Close runs between the gables. According to legend, Peter Williamson was imprisoned here. Other temporary prisons were said to be at Aedie's House on the other side of the wynd, in nearby Rennie's Wynd and even in the tolbooth itself.

THE OPEN-AIR MARKET

*

Throughout the nineteenth century the Green continued to thrive with numerous residents, some professions, many trades and a few industries; an optician, a surgeon-apothecary and an accountant; grocers and spirit dealers, drapers, a pork curer, baker, druggist, tea dealer, hairdresser, straw bonnet makers, umbrella makers, cabinet-maker, a ginger-beer and porter dealer, stoneware and fancy goods merchants. The golden teapot, the sign of John Adams, tea merchant, at No. 64, near Ædie's Lodging, was an enduring landmark for years. The poet William Anderson and the journalist William Carnie were born in the Green. Alexander Rhind, an early partner of John Crombie, the wool manufacturer, had a tannery, kiln, comb shop and dungstead nearby.

It was argued that Union Street, laid out by 1805, would finish off the

The Green in the 1890s, looking east to the formidable bulk of Archibald Simpson's New Market.

13

Green. Instead, opportunists among the tradesmen there hoisted signs advertising their skills to passers-by in Union Street before its houses were built. The other side of the coin was that 'idle and disorderly persons' in Union Street could throw 'offensive matter' down the chimneys of the Green dwellers. It was said that the New Market of 1842 would toll the death knell of the Green. It had the reverse effect. Access to the Green was made easier, for one could walk straight there from the basement of the New Market, or approach it from the new streets, Market and Hadden, or by the Back Wynd Stairs (the dangerous originals were replaced in 1922 by the present stairs). By the late nineteenth century there were fishwives with creels (who were still there into the twentieth century), butchers' stalls, linen sales and furniture salesmen, as well as the usual dairy produce, flowers, fruit and plants.

In 1870, William Cadenhead wrote in *Olden Days in Aberdeen*:

> I recollect when potatoes could be bought at 3d per old peck and that was a good carry; eggs at 4d to 6d per dozen; butter at 7d to 9d per lb, not a trifling 16oz pound but a decent lump, weighing 28 ounces.

DEMOLITIONS AND NEAR-DISASTER

*

Though the open-air market was not affected by the building up of Union Street, the Green lost its importance as a major route into town when the Bow Brig was removed in 1851 and its character on the north side changed with the development of the big Union Street stores, which had rear entrances at Green level. Like the Langstane Place section of the Hardgate, it had become a back lane for a section of Union Street's south side. The original medieval houses, which had become rundown, were demolished. Ædie's Lodging, its ground floor occupied by two shops, was the last original house to go, in 1914. It was so narrow that it could accommodate Nos 127–31 Union Street behind it. Its site at the foot of the Back Wynd Stairs has never been built over. Across Ædie's Wynd, the twin gable-ended 'Peter Williamson' houses were demolished when Boots the Chemist opened in Union Street in 1936 with its lower levels on the Green, custom-built in a simple art deco style by George Bennet Mitchell & Son, architects.

By the post-war era not only were the buildings on the south side suffering from neglect but Littlewoods was given permission to build back from Union Street over the Green to extend floor space. A structure on stilts resembling a series of portacabins piled on top of one another emerged at the west end.

During the 1980s and early '90s a flurry of schemes for the redevelopment of the area emerged, the worst being a joint proposal of Wimpey Properties, Woolworths and Boots which entailed the complete covering in of the Green. The traders, most of them long-established, among them the Brochies of Feughside, Coutts of Bograxie, Coplands of Alford, the Mairs of Tarves, Mr Smith of Lyne of Skene, the Pennys of Cove Bay, the Davidsons of Whitehouse and Mr William Gordon were concerned about the uncertainty of the situation and there was anger in the city that a truly historic area was being sacrificed to increase chain-store floor space. Fortunately this plan did not go ahead. Another massive scheme evaporated when the leading developers suffered financial reverses and Boots and Woolworths decided to pitch their tent in the new Bon Accord Centre. A much smaller scheme was mooted in 1992, and the south side was sympathetically reconstructed. The market, alas, is not what it was.

The Green in the 1900s looking west, before the erection of the Littlewood's extension, showing the old buildings of the south side.

THE TRINITY FRIARS' PLACE

*

At the east end of the Green a little lane called Fisher Row, which survived well into the nineteenth century, led to 'the street called Trinity Corner'. Here stood the monastery of the Trinity Friars close by the quay, with the waters of the Denburn estuary lapping at its dykes at high tide. Hector Boece, first principal of King's College stated in his *History of Scotland*, 1526, that King William the Lion, near the time of his death in 1211, gifted the recently founded Order of the Holy Trinity 'his palace riall in Aberdene to big [build] thair abbaye'. The legend has endured even though the existence of this royal palace has never been proved. Whatever the truth, the Trinitarians' chapel, with its slender spire, was for long one of the landmarks of the harbour area and the friars' flower garden and orchard was famed in Aberdeen.

At the time of the Reformation the Trinity Friars' monastery was looted and set on fire by the 'reforming' mob. The worst outrage recorded took place here when an elderly monk, Friar Francis, was stabbed while attempting to save the monastery's treasures and his body thrown into the flames.

A vignette from Parson Gordon's Plan, 1661. In line with the ploughman is the chapel of the Trinity Friars (19) and the shaded area to the right with the sailing ship is the Denburn estuary. Centre (12) is St Catherine's Hill with the houses of the Shiprow on the right-hand slope. The tall spire, left, is that of the tolbooth.

THE KIRKYARD AS SHIPYARD
*

The monastery buildings lay in ruins for years, but in 1606 were acquired by Andrew Davidson, a 'tymberman' from St Andrews who had 'bocht the Wood of Drum' at least 'as much it as will big ane bark' (build a ship). The logs were to be floated down the River Dee from Drum and the proximity of the monastery's burial ground to the harbour estuary made it an ideal choice for a shipyard, if perhaps not for a royal palace. Unfortunately over the years the Trinitarians' kirkyard had become 'filithie abusit' with middens and the rubbish had to be cleared first. The good ship *Bon-Accord* was launched from the Trinity kirkyard-shipyard on 28 July 1609 and would have sailed down what is the lower part of Guild Street on her maiden voyage. That brings us to the remarkable personality who gave his name to Guild Street.

DR WILLIAM GUILD AND TRINITY HALL
*

The shipyard appears to have been a 'one-off' venture, and in 1631 the old monastery complex was acquired by Dr William Guild, city minister, zealot, opportunist, principal of King's and of Marischal College, brother-in-law of Davy-do-a'thing and benefactor of the Seven Incorporated Trades of Aberdeen. He was the son of Matthew Guild, armourer and deacon of the Hammermen Craft of the Incorporated Trades. Dr Guild had the ruinous buildings repaired and in honour of his late father, gifted them to the Incorporated Trades who had no meeting place of their own. They named their new headquarters Trinity Hall or Tarnty Ha, in memory of the friars. It was quite a splendid place, a two-storey L-plan building, with a projecting wing tower with a corbelled angle turret, in the style of Andrew Jamesone, though a little late to be his work. The meeting hall was sixty-four feet long; lit by seven windows, it had brass chandeliers and a fireplace at each end, and was furnished with oak chairs and paintings which remain among the Trades' greatest treasures. Another former monastery building became the Trades' Hospital, home to 'decayit craftsmen' but, becoming 'decayit' itself, was replaced by a new neo-classical hospital around 1790. This building was later used as the Trades' School.

Members of the Trades usually worshipped in St Nicholas Kirk, so from 1703 the redundant monastery chapel was rented out to Episcopalians. It presently became ruinous and after its demolition in 1794 the site was acquired by a breakaway section of the East Kirk's congregation who built

*Trinity Corner, 1830. In the foreground is the magnificent gateway commemorating
Dr Guild's benefaction, and behind it, partially hidden, is Trinity Hall. Right,
the new Trades Hospital and left, Trinity Church.*

Trinity Chapel of Ease, later Trinity Church there. When the Aberdeen
Railway was projected in 1844, the plans indicated that the Trinity Corner site
would be required for its station. Although the railway plans came to naught,
the Trades had prudently acquired a feu at the south-east corner of Union
Bridge and commissioned the city architect, John Smith, to design a splendid
new Trinity Hall. Here they moved in 1846, taking their ornate gateway with
them. It was not until 1857 that the end of the line came for the old Trinity
Friars' Place, demolished to make way for the development of Guild Street
and Exchange Street. Trinity Church survived. It luckily stood in the line of
Guild Street, was incorporated, and re-emerged in 1867 as the Alhambra
Music Hall. After the building of the nearby Tivoli (as Her Majesty's) in 1873,
the Alhambra closed and re-emerged again as a shop, and now as a Chinese
takeaway, at Nos 12–14 Guild Street, on the corner with Exchange Street. This
is exactly the site of the original chapel of the Trinity Friars.

This photograph shows Trinity Hall still standing (centre), but the demolition of the Trades' Hospital, right, is under way. The Chapel of Ease, later Trinity Church, is left rear, with its manse in front. Centre, William Smith's new Guild Street goods station and railway offices tower aloft.

Trinity Quay looking west to Guild Street, 1949. From right, Shore Brae at the junction with Trinity Quay. Weigh-House Square is just beyond, out of shot. Directly opposite, a ship is moored at the site of the ancient Quay or Keyhead. A lorry negotiates Market Street at the Guild Street intersection, and, left, the Guild Street goods station, demolished in 2003 for extensive redevelopment. Above the square tower of St John's Episcopal Church, still there (see page 44); Extreme left, A. R. Gray Ltd's handsome warehouse of 1885, demolished in 1973 and replaced by a modern office block.

THE TOWN'S WEIGH-HOUSE

✳

The right to levy all goods for sale within Aberdeen by weighing and measuring, and to gain some useful revenue thereby, was conferred on the community (i.e. the magistrates), by King Robert the Bruce in the famous charter of 1319. It was not all plain sailing. The right was later re-conferred by James IV on Admiral James Wood in a troublesome charter and then claimed in 1585, through purchase, by Alexander Rutherford. By 1617 the magistrates felt it high time to reassert their own rights and bought Rutherford off with 1,000 merks, in return for his acknowledgement of the superiority of the town's claim by virtue of King Robert's charter. Things eventually got underway in 1634 when a weigh-house or packhouse was built near the quay. It was an ideal position, well placed for goods arriving via the Bow Brig as well as those unloaded from the quay. It was a long building of rough undressed blocks. The walls were three feet thick and the slated roof was steep-pitched, with tiny garret windows.

The weigh-house sat back from the road to allow space for goods and weighing machines. In Parson Gordon's time it was known as the packhouse because it contained equipment for packing woollen cloth and stockings prior to export to the continent. An additional 'wing', a lean-to building, slopes away to the right, with steps leading up to it. The railing was for tethering horses. Trinity and Regent Quays later developed on either side. Stand at the top of the Shiprow today and look left, across to the Harbour Office. That was where the weigh-house stood.

The weighing machine or 'tron' (not a common word in Aberdeen), with weights and measures supplied by the Dean of Guild, was rouped to the highest bidder, who as tacksman carried out the weighing and measuring on behalf of the town, pocketed the levy (later known as the bell and petty customs) and expected to make some profit, while the magistrates acquired ready money and were saved the trouble of carrying out the task themselves. Dues were set at a fixed rate: at one time, pork and beef at a penny per hundredweight, feathers at 2d a stone, and up to six firlots of meal at 4d. Other commodities levied included butter, cheese, rough fat, tallow, stockings, plaiding, down, coal, and iron.

After being in existence for twenty years or so, the weigh-house was so overcrowded that a 'toofall' or lean-to building was added at the rear. Aberdeen Shore Works accounts for 1658–9 record the purchase of considerable quantities of stones, trees (wooden posts), nails, slates, pins, lime, joists, sand, pinings and iron, for its erection at a total cost of £257 4s 3d. Scots. The area around the weigh-house offered plenty of room for produce and merchandise awaiting the attention of the weighman, but a hard, quick-drying, mud-free surface was essential for the stacking of sacks, packs and barrels. The accounts for the following year show that considerable quantities of small stones and sand were 'led' or carted to the quayside and various sums paid out 'for cassying the [pack]hous'. The forestairs and a balcony were added in 1707, the flooring of the latter thriftily made from timbers recovered from a Levant galley out of Amsterdam wrecked at the Black Dog. It was replaced in 1814 by the cast-iron balcony shown opposite. Merchants would sell direct from the weigh-house to save transport costs. In October 1791 an advertisement appeared in the *Aberdeen Journal*:

Apples, just arrived in excellent condition for baking and table, 4/6 a barrel. Can be seen in the well-frequented loft at the back of the Weigh-House. Apply to William Anderson, Gallowgate, John Reid, Netherkirkgate, Alexander Symmers, Broadgate.

From an advertisement of June 1794, one learns that, by order of the magistrates, an area has been set aside at the east end of the weigh-house for the woolmarket. 'Country people will ... have the benefit of the weigh-house lodging for their wool overnight.' The woolmarket previously held beside the Market Cross had been prohibited as 'very inconvenient'.

There was a lost property department for all sorts of merchandise whose owners could not be traced; chests of tea, indigo, bales of wool, oranges, bundles of hoops, toys, crockery, bars of iron and steel. After a year and a day these goods could be sold to the highest bidder. Packages could not be opened in advance and the buyer had to take pot luck. When the bell and petty customs was abolished in 1879, there was no further official use for the weighhouse. The loft was then used for storing sails and the ground floor acted as a potato and hay store. Latterly the premises were let out to joiners and other tradesmen. It was demolished in 1883 and the handsome Harbour Office was built on the site.

THE SHIPROW

*

The Schipraw or Shiprow or *vicus navium*, the road of the ships, was first mentioned in a charter of 1281 and grew in importance along with the Castlegate. It was a stage in the road from the south, and, via Shore Brae, the road from the quay, the harbour and even the continent. Persons of quality lived in the area. Lord Forbes' townhouse was at Putachieside before it became a slum. Robert Davidson, provost of Aberdeen from 1405–8 and again in 1410, had a tavern in the Shiprow as well as an involvement in organised piracy with Alexander Stewart, Earl of Mar, his business partner and comrade-in-arms at 'Reid [red] Harlaw'. Davidson was slain at the battle, the only provost of Aberdeen to die in defence of the burgh so far.

St Catherine's Chapel, 'by ancient report' (according to the historian William Kennedy) was dedicated to St Catherine of Sienna and established on the summit in 1242 by John Kennedy, Constable of Aberdeen. St Catherine of Sienna's dates were roughly 1347–80 so this was indeed a miracle.

Life in the Shiprow was not entirely blissful. In the sixteenth century there was a feud between the chaplains of St Catherine's backed by the magistrates, and a resident, John Chalmer, who persisted in obstructing a passage between the Green and the chapel by building across it. In 1648 the residents were given permission to enclose St Catherine's Hill with dykes to keep out 'whoors, shankwyvers [probably idlers rather than honest stocking knitters] and horrsis'. In 1669, several houses were burned down by a great fire at the head of the Shiprow while others were pulled down to prevent it spreading. The town council ordered a special collection at church doors for the relief of the sufferers. It may have been after the fire that the Shiprow Port, perhaps damaged, was re-positioned above Shore Brae. Its position below had allowed enemies and other undesirables disembarking at the quay and turning right at the top of Shore Brae to arrive in the Castlegate unimpeded.

BURNETT'S LODGING

*

The houses on the west side of the Shiprow curving down to the quay were high and handsome in their heyday. The upper rooms offered an excellent view of the embryonic harbour, and their long gardens stretched back to St Catherine's Chapel, though it lay in ruins after the Reformation. One of the

Burnett's Lodging sat at the end of Jamieson's Court, a narrow pend at No. 40 Shiprow. Old Landmarks of Aberdeen, *G. Gordon Burr, 1885.*

finest houses was Burnett's Lodging, near the top of the brae, an L-shaped backhouse, three storeys high, with a corbelled-out stair turret.

A feature of the finest houses in the Shiprow and elsewhere, as already noted, was the marriage stone, but No. 40 had two. Just as well, for one, dated 1634, went missing. It graced an attic dormer of No. 40 Shiprow and bore the initials A. B. (Alexander Burnett) and I. C. (perhaps his wife Isabella, one of the Shiprow Chalmers). Another stone was inscribed 'AB' and '16', and combined the coat of arms of the Burnetts – three holly leaves with a hunting horn – with the lion rampant. It now sits at the rear of the Maritime Museum, rather confusingly labelled 'The Adelphi Stone'.

PROVOST ROSS'S HOUSE AND ITS NEIGHBOURS
✳

Heading down the Shiprow, we come to Nos 44–6 which Andrew Jamesone built for his colleague Robert Watson, wright and burgess. It had the Jamesone hallmarks: it was three-storeys high with a projecting, gabled wing. Watson's initials and those of his wife Margaret Collie and the date of building, 1593, were on the skewputts and skew stones. Several well-heeled owners followed and in 1702 the house was acquired by the merchant John Ross of Arnage, provost of Aberdeen from 1710–11. It endured many trials and tribulations before it was christened Provost Ross's House in the mid-twentieth century.

Next door, Nos 48–50, another fine house, had a double arcade, Abbey Place, which led to a little court of that name. There was no abbey, though there may have been confusion with the chapel. The date 1710 is still visible on the capital of the central column of the double arcade. Both houses suffered years of neglect and go into the 'almost lost' category. Continuing downhill, there were two further good houses, then came Nos 62–4 a very fine townhouse which faced down Shore Brae. It had a harled frontage and roll-moulded surrounds to the main door and small-paned windows. An oval shield within a strapwork cartouche in a square frame of freestone above the door gives the date 1692 with initials I. S. and C. E. It was demolished in 1876 to make way for the new Trinity Congregational Church, architect James Matthews, whose name recalled the ancient Trinity Friars. Its two neighbours above were taken down later.

The creation of Union Street in 1801–5 marked the beginning of the end for the Shiprow. Even before the demographic drift west, the street was mutilated by topping and tailing. St Catherine's Hill was partly beheaded to make

Once handsome Shiprow houses slope down to the quay. Top, Provost Ross's, right and Abbey Place. Their neighbour, with a frontage of light, squared granite, is glimpsed. The rear of the new ABC Cinema, The Regal, looms above. The Shiprow Tavern (the old Union Church) is extreme right. Below left, is another tall house with pedimented dormers and small-paned windows. Below right, demolition has already started on the 'very fine' Nos 62-64 opposite Shore Brae. The four protruding tusks above the policeman's helmet may have been a remnant of the Shiprow Port after it was re positioned. A few passers-by have gathered to assist the photographer. The postman and telegraph boy have taken a moment off from their labours at new Post Office which opened a year earlier, in 1875, at the foot of Market Street.

a flat surface for the new street, and the remaining sand on the east side was sold off by the sackload. That part of the Shiprow which curved round to join the Netherkirkgate was erased by Union Street. A tiny rump survives on the north side and as St Catherine's Wynd leads off between the two Esslemont & Mackintosh stores into the Netherkirkgate.

The laying out of Market Street in 1842 truncated the lower section of the Shiprow. It comes to a sudden end near the foot of the east side of Market Street, between the former Douglas Hotel and the side of the Post Office of 1875, now various offices, but still remembered as 'The Brew' (the old Labour Exchange). Trinity Lane on the other side of Market Street is the continuation of the Shiprow and leads into the Green. By the later nineteenth century the merchants were going west and their Shiprow houses went over to multiple occupation, while their long gardens gave way to slum housing.

Burnett's Lodging and other buildings on the upper part of the west side of the Shiprow were demolished by the late 1930s. With the lower houses already gone, Provost Ross's and Abbey Place stood in dangerous isolation. Rescue came in the unlikely form of Associated British Cinemas (ABC) who planned a cinema near the Union Street/Shiprow corner and had acquired the houses for conversion to a staff residence. Plans were shelved at the outbreak of war and by 1945 the houses were almost ruinous, having suffered badly from fire damage caused by squatters. ABC donated the buildings to the city along with £6,500 towards restoration. There were those in Aberdeen who felt these ruins were worthless and their restoration a waste of money. The property was subsequently acquired by the National Trust for Scotland and demolition by the town council was prevented. In 1973 Fenton Wyness wrote dramatically in *More Spots from the Leopard:*

> Some twenty years ago when the suggestion was made to retain and restore Aberdeen's oldest dwelling – the building now known as Provost Ross's House in the Shiprow – it touched off one of the most bitter controversies the city had known for many years. Looking back, it was an unsavoury battle, waged with all the petty rancour of local party politics – a typical reaction when any attempt is made to save the city's precious patrimony. However the building was eventually saved, though only by a few hours, a surreptitious plot to pull it down having been outmanoeuvred.

By 1954 Provost Ross's and Abbey Place (both now lumped together as Provost Ross's House) had been restored for the National Trust for Scotland by the architect A. G. R. Mackenzie. Hailed now as 'a gem of seventeenth-century architecture', this 'architectural group of unusual interest' was opened to the public. In 1984 the Aberdeen Maritime Museum was based at Provost Ross's House and was further expanded in 1996 by the addition of the now-disused Trinity Congregational Church down the brae, the two united by a glass frontage.

THE EAST SIDE
*

The Union Church had been built there in 1882 as a Chapel of Ease for the East Parish. It lay at a lower level and was reached by steps. In 1932 the now-disused church was acquired by the Temperance Association who re-opened

Though this illustration focuses on Provost Ross's House, it gives a glimpse of the more modest houses on the east side. The entrance to Shore Brae is beside the thatched cottage. Aberdeen in Byegone Days, *Robert Anderson, 1910.*

The Union Church, later the Shiprow Tavern.

it as the Shiprow Tavern, its name boldly painted so as to be visible from the top of the brae. It provided warmth, company, billiards and tasty meals for men with nowhere to go but the streets. It was demolished by 1960, along with the rest of the east side, though the Tavern relocated to Constitution Street.

EXCHEQUER ROW

*

And so from the Schipraw to the Chackraw, alias 'le chekery' or the Chekar, as Exchequer Row used to be called, quite a few names for a short, narrow street where little sunlight penetrated the tall buildings. It linked the Shiprow and the Castlegate, and the south side had four closes which ran towards the quay.

'Le chekery' is first recorded in the mid-fourteenth century. Robert the Bruce's second daughter, Matilda, was married to an Aberdeen burgess, Thomas Isaacs, possibly the town clerk, and they lived there until her death in 1353. Another glimpse of Exchequer Row's high-class past is the offering for sale at the Market Cross in 1448 of a 'litil sclate house' (a cut above your

Right.
Exchequer Row from the Shiprow, looking through to the Castlegate, with the
Market Cross and the Citadel in the distance. The houses on the south or
right-hand side fronted the long closes leading down towards the quay.

'hedder-thackit' biggings) 'liand in the Chekar' along with another, to 'ony that wald b[u]y thaim and gif maist for thaim'.

There were two reasons for 'le chekery's' prestige. Here, the king's custom house was located, where the local accounts of the royal customs gatherers were audited. The name Chackraw derived from the Latin *scaccarium* or *skakkarium*, a chequerboard, an early reckoning aid. (Desks laid out in this way with black and white checks known as 'counters'). Secondly, one of the royal mints of Scotland was based in Aberdeen, possibly in the 'Chekar', for in 1799 an oak panel, showing the arms of James V (1513–44) with the initials V. R. for William Rolland, the Master of the Mint, was removed from one of its oldest houses. The Rollands, lairds of Disblair, were one of the merchant burgess families of Aberdeen; their wealth came from the Danzig trade. Dr William Guild had married Catherine Rolland in 1610. The mint issued coins, mainly silver groats, from Alexander III's reign until the early sixteenth century.

Extreme left, the former Bank of Scotland, with the Athenaeum building opposite. These remain. Between them stand the tall houses on the south side of Exchequer Row and the Castlegate. The Bursars' House (which follows) is third from the Bank, with Nos 1–3 Exchequer Row beyond. Detail from Hay's Print of the Castlegate, 1840.

Though its exact site is unknown, the area around Stronach's Close, sometimes advertised as being off Castle Street (the borderline was vague), is favoured. Robert Stronach himself was a wright, whose eccentricity was to gather shells tossed up on the beach after storms and decorate the walls of his house with them. 'Shally's', as the Close was nicknamed, had genteel residents, including at one time the artist Robert Seaton. Dancing master Robert Dun held his class there, including instruction in the evening for gentlemen who were unable to come during the day.

Nos 1–3 Exchequer Row was an eighteenth-century, three-storey house with a frontage of coursed granite ashlar with two windows, a door and a pend, all arcaded. The pend gave access to Burnett's Close which took its name from the merchant Robert Burnett of Elrick, burgess of Aberdeen from 1685. His townhouse, with its coat-of-arms panel dated 1669, stood at the end of this very long close. The house was latterly known as Exchequer Place, 'place' indicating a house or group of houses of quality. From the early nineteenth century it became home to Affleck's Tavern, a famous eating place with a vaulted wine cellar.

Exchequer Row degenerated into an over-crowded, disease-ridden slum and its demolition, instigated on health grounds by Professor Matthew Hay, Aberdeen's Medical Officer of Health, was sanctioned in 1895 under the

Exchequer Row does service as a tour stance after the demolitions of 1952. The ogee gable and garret windows of Menzies' back-house (page 37) peep over a wall, left.

Housing of the Working Classes Act and carried out in 1902. When Robert Burnett's house was demolished, a secret passage running from its cellar to the shore was discovered. In the seventeenth and eighteenth centuries smuggling had been blatantly carried on around Aberdeen and the town's magistrates were among those involved. Never again would small boats laden with contraband tie up at the quay beside the entrance to Burnett's secret passage! The remaining buildings in this area were taken down in 1952.

THE BURSARS' HOUSE

*

Exchequer Row and the adjoining houses on the south-west side of the Castlegate were part of the same terrace and the latter were also demolished during the clearance programmes. Only the building at Nos 55–7 Castlegate, with the Titled Wig pub on the ground floor (formerly the Lang Bar, the Saloon, and the Welly Boot), survives from this group, the upper floor giving an inkling of the long-gone elegance of the terrace. Among those taken down was the Bursars' House at Nos 60–1, the last of the Castlegate group. Dating from the sixteenth century it had originally been the property of the Rollands, though Dr William Guild had acquired it from his in-laws in 1636. He described it as his 'forehouse in the Castellgate wherein I dwell [with] brew house, with rooms above, in the other side of the close'. He died there in 1657.

Guild bequeathed his house to the Seven Incorporated Trades, not as a lodging for bursars, but as a source of income in the form of mails (rents) to support three of them, sons of poor craftsmen, at Marischal College. The lads had to show some academic ability and be, as Guild put it, 'able for the said colledge'. In 1884 the Trades received dispensation to sell and the Bursars' House became a pub, the Bursars' Hotel. It was demolished in 1902.

The Shiprow Tavern and its neighbours were replaced by an ugly multi-storey carpark. The site of Exchequer Row and the Bursars' House was covered by a Grandfare supermarket, which became 'What Every Woman Wants'. Both have closed and massive redevelopment as an entertainment complex is contemplated.

CHAPTER 2

THE CASTLEGATE

We have arrived in the heart of Aberdeen at last, the much-admired civic square. Though the street signs say 'Castle Street', people still refer to the great square as 'The Castlegate'. 'Street' seems too mundane. The enigmatic castle itself had vanished by the time the Castlegate was blossoming, but it did not matter in the least that it was the 'gate' or road to something that no longer existed. As Daniel Defoe wrote:

> The great market place is very beautiful and spacious, and the Streets adjoining are very handsome and well built, the Houses lofty and high. Built not so as to be inconvenient, as in Edinburgh: or low, to be contemptible as in most other places.
> *Tour thro' the Whole Island of Great Britain* (1724–7)

The Castlegate was the place of entertainment, with capital and corporal punishments by various means, and markets and shows, which Aberdonians loved. In December 1792 Mr Fosco's Collection of Wild Beasts was advertised:

> A very curious Porcupine from the coast of Barbary, the Ethiopian or Savage or Hairy man, a very ravenous Wolf, the American monster, and many more. At the Market Place of Castle Street.

We can walk anti-clockwise round the Castlegate, ending at Broad Street, the start of the way out of town. Before beginning the tour, the shop of the merchant John Ewen is worth a visit.

Ewen started out as a packman from Montrose and became prosperous enough to own land in Ferryhill and property in the Castlegate. Here he sold silverware, jewellery, shoe buckles, tooth powder, fowling pieces, German flutes, coats of arms, telescopes and screwdrivers. His shop was a collection point for donations for the bereaved and destitute, for the new infirmary and for the ransom of local mariners captured by Barbary pirates. He was secre-

33

This is another version of the cover of this book, drawn by Hugh, one of the Irvines of Drum, showing the Castlegate in 1813, looking west. The plinth of the Mannie Well (William Lindsay, 1710), extreme right and the Market Cross (John Montgomerie, Old Rayne, 1686), rear, on the left, are still with us, though they have changed places. The former Aberdeen Bank, (James Burn of Haddington, 1800) left rear, with prominent cornice is the third great Castlegate survivor. Everything else has gone, including John Ewen's shop behind the Market Cross.

John Ewen's shop was on the ground floor of the house with the gablet behind the Market Cross. Detail from Irvine's View of the Castlegate.

tary for the 'reform of the internal government of Scots burghs', which in these 'unreformed' days was self-electing, the author of the Police Act of 1795 and among Aberdeen's first police commissioners. He organised Sunday schools and bathing machines at the Beach; he was a poet and one of the literary coterie around the poet, James Beattie, professor of Moral Philosophy at Marischal College, and was a patron of local artists including two neighbours, Robert Seaton and the miniaturist, Andrew Robertson, whom he placed under the tuition of Nasymth in Edinburgh and paid the fees. He seems to have done almost everything except write *The Boatie Rows*, which was at one time attributed to him. He died in 1821 leaving £14,000, a fortune for the time. The Athenaeum, Archibald Simpson, 1822, was built on the site of Ewen's shop the year after his death, linking up with the already extant Union Buildings to the west. Indeed, this splendid project was held up because Simpson could not get access to the site until Ewen's death.

THE SOUTH SIDE

THE EARL MARISCHAL'S LODGING AND THE LAIRD OF PITFODELS' HOUSE

*

The Earl Marischal's Lodging, a towerhouse, had a courtyard to the rear and a garden extending southwards towards the quay. Legend has it that it was from a window overlooking the Castlegate that Marischal's son-in-law, the Earl of Moray, the future regent of Scotland, forced his half-sister, Mary Queen of Scots, to watch the messy execution of her aspiring lover, Bonnie John Gordon after the Battle of Corrichie of 1562. It was from the forestairs of the courtyard in 1638 that covenanting ministers preached when the doors of St Nicholas Kirk were locked against them by the magistrates. Aberdonians were not impressed:

> *From Dickson, Henderson and Cant,*
> *Apostles of the Covenant,*
> *Good Lord deliver us*

It was at the Earl Marischal's Lodging that Jacobite leaders gathered in February 1716 to learn that the Old Pretender had fled.

Pitfodels' Lodging, next door to the west, was owned by the powerful Catholic family, the Menzies of Pitfodels, who held the provostship of

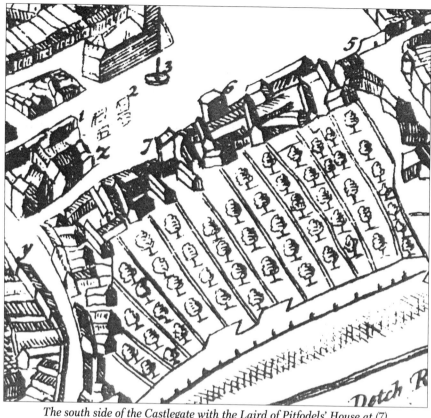

*The south side of the Castlegate with the Laird of Pitfodels' House at (7)
and Earl Marischal's Lodging at (6). These two sixteenth-century houses were the
finest in Aberdeen in their time. Unfortunately pictorial records are poor.
This detail from Parson Gordon's Plan is the best we have.*

Aberdeen eleven times between 1423 and 1635. In 1533, Gilbert, the incumbent
Menzies, replaced his wooden house there with this fine 'stane hoose', one of
the earliest in Aberdeen. It was turreted and three storeys high, probably the
work of Deacon William Jamesone, father of Andrew the mason and grandfather of the artist George. It was here that Gilbert's son, Provost Thomas
Menzies, entertained King James V when he visited Aberdeen in 1537. The
visit was marked by a splendid heraldic carving, the Royal Arms of Scotland
displayed over those of Menzies of Pitfodels. Charles II and his entourage
had a hastily arranged stay here in July 1650 en route from Holland to
Charles's coronation at Scone. The king was 'attended by a female friend', his
current mistress, Catherine Pegge. Great crowds gathered in the Castlegate
hoping they might catch a glimpse of royal hochmagandies. The local ministers, worried that such behaviour might undermine the morals of their flocks,

sent one of their number to ask the king to draw the curtains.

There were occasional petty squabbles between the neighbouring grandees. In December 1595 George, fourth Earl and founder of Marischal College, took Gilbert Menzies to court to force him to repair a ruinous wall next to his lodging. Gilbert replied that if the Earl's property had suffered 'skaith', 'the same is his ain default by the casting of ane gutter'.

The Earl Marischal was attainted after his participation in the Jacobite Rising of 1715 and the great house fell into disuse. The idea of a 'fine new street', wider and less arduous to climb than the Shiprow, giving a direct approach to the increasingly busy quay was successfully mooted in civic and mercantile circles. The site of the Earl's abandoned property, if demolished, would offer an ideal access so the Aberdeen magistrates bought 'his Lordship's Lodging' and garden for £803 13s 4d in 1767. Thus, Marischal Street was created and named in his honour. It was the main thoroughfare between harbour and town until 1840 when Market Street was laid out.

Menzies of Pitfodels' Back-house

*

The family lodging had passed to John Menzies, 7th of Pitfodels but he disposed of his property when the laying out of Marischal Street was under consideration. It languished for a time, and the rooms were rented out to various schools and as a venue for book auctions. Francis Peacock, the burgh's dancing master, held classes in Pitfodels' Lodging, below John Ross's schoolroom before he acquired Skipper Scott's Close (later, of course, Peacock's). The end came on 26 June 1799 when a contractor was advertised for in the *Aberdeen Journal*, to take down 'that house on the south side of Castle Street, Aberdeen, formerly called Pitfodels' Lodging.' The great kitchen and its arched fireplace were still intact when the building was demolished. The handsome Aberdeen Bank was built in 1800 on the site of Pitfodels' Lodging. Subsequent to its crash in 1848 it was acquired by the Union Bank which later merged with the Bank of Scotland, whose Aberdeen head office it became. It was converted to a court house during 2004–5.

Menzies had built a back-house for himself at the rear of his property to designs by William Adam. It had an ogee–moulded central gablet containing three attic windows with an oval oculus (small window) above (page 31). Here the heraldic panel marking James V's visit was preserved and in 1806 it was moved again when the Menzies family took it with them to a 'modern' house in Belmont Street. The Castlegate back-house was demolished in 1965.

37

THE MARISCHAL STREET
DEMOLITIONS
*

Marischal Street was laid out between 1767 and 1793. It was a Georgian street of gracious townhouses with elegant interiors, built by skilled master masons. Two-thirds of the way down, the single-arch Bannerman's Bridge flyover, named after its mason and built to designs of William Law, spanned the newly laid-out Virginia Street below. It was the first of its kind in Scotland.

Bannerman's Bridge over Virginia Street awaits the end. The turret, right, belongs to the Shore Porters' Virginia Street building. Left, Nos 36 and 38 Marischal Street from the rear, already under demolition.

Top, Nos 36 and 38 and below, Nos 39 and 40a Marischal Street prior to demolition.

As property in and around Union Street became increasingly fashionable Marischal Street went down in the world and it was not until the 1970s that it began to be appreciated again. Virginia Street was due to be widened to form part of an inner ring road. This apparently necessitated the demolition of Bannerman's Bridge, still in sound condition, and the two houses immediately north, Nos 39 and 40a to the east and Nos 36 and 38 to the west to accommodate a wider bridge.

To emphasise the unique value of Marischal Street, Aberdeen Civic Society published a detailed survey of its houses with notes on its distinguished residents. The north-east branch of the Georgian Society, as it then was, set out alternative routes for Virginia Street, even designs for a tunnel, obviating the need for taking down the houses. Such plans were turned down. Since the scheme involved the demolition of listed buildings in a conservation area, a public inquiry was instituted by the Secretary of State for Scotland in 1973. Consent to demolish was granted subject to the proviso that local residents should be satisfied and that the final reconstruction with reclaimed granite facings should be 'aesthetically pleasing', which seemed somehow to miss the point. It was 1983 before the demolitions were carried out.

St Clement's Manse
*

Before Bannerman's Bridge was demolished one could look across to a mid-eighteenth-century gem, the Manse of St Clement's Kirk at No. 23½ Virginia Street. It was approached by a pend, a long flight of steps, garden and gateway. A short flight of shaped granite steps with iron handrails took one to the front door which was flanked by Ionic pilasters with entablature and a dentilled pediment. The frontage, of granite with sandstone dressed work, had several fine features including ogee skew moulding at the centre gablet and a granite rear stair tower. In spite of attempts to preserve it, the manse was demolished in 1975 even though it sat above the line of the widened Virginia Street.

Right.
St Clement's Manse, Virginia Street, centre, with a stunning view
of the vanished back houses on the south side of the Castlegate.
The fairytale towers of the Salvation Army Citadel, top, remain.

The manse retained remnants of its former glory till the end. This room had an internal décor of rococo panels and a scalloped-shelved buffet niche.

ROLLAND'S LODGING
*

Back up in the Castlegate again, Rolland's Lodging, a sixteenth-century house of intriguing aspect, lay near the east end of the south side. Its twin gables are shown on the extreme left of Irvine's view, facing onto the Castlegate, though old folk remember it being less lofty in reality than Irvine indicates. It was originally the town lodging of the mintmasters, the Rollands of Disblair.

It was extended around 1630 and by 1704 was in the ownership of Sir Samuel Forbes of Foveran, author of the *Description of Aberdeenshire*. Rolland's Lodging, No. 36 Castle Street, eventually became a tenement with a fruit wholesaler and a furniture store occupying the ground floors for many years, both of whom may have found the original vaulted cellars below useful as storage. When the lodging was demolished in 1935, the arched fireplaces, pine panelling and wall aumbries of the first-floor rooms were still intact, reminders of gracious living.

Rolland's Lodging, some time after 1842 when the Market Cross was re-sited at the east end of the Castlegate. The westerly gable of Rolland's was a clothier's shop at this time and garments for sale are pegged outside in the traditional manner. The shop of the merchant George Stratton was on the ground floor of the building, extreme left.

St John's Court

✳

The pend between the two gables of Rolland's Lodging led through to No. 38 Castlegate, St John's Court. The name came from a chapel built on the east side of the court in the 1780s by the Rev. Roger Aitken of St John's Scottish Episcopalian Church. This was one of several meeting houses the congregation occupied before they finally settled in St John's Place. The manse, with a hipped roof, sat to the rear of the chapel.

In 1899 the premises were purchased by the Association for Improving the Condition of the Poor as its headquarters and were entered through the pend. The charity was renamed the Aberdeen Association of Social Service in 1947 and later, Voluntary Service, Aberdeen. The frontage has been redeveloped in a modern idiom and manse and chapel followed the fate of Rolland's Lodging.

St John's Court behind Rolland's Lodging. The chapel is left of the manse.

CASTLE TERRACE:
NOS 6–8 CASTLE TERRACE
✳

The south side of the Castlegate ended a few yards east of Rolland's Lodging and round the corner was Castle Terrace. On the far side of the road was a sternly handsome townhouse dating from 1720. It had started life in Hangman's Brae, later known less gruesomely as Castle Brae, and later still, in 1864, became Nos 6–8 Castle Terrace when the Brae was absorbed by the Terrace. It overlooked the harbour, reminding its owner Dr Patrick Blaikie of his days as a naval surgeon. He had been aboard the *HMS Undaunted* which took Napoleon into exile on Elba in 1814. 'While with us he did not appear depressed,' Blaikie wrote to his father John Blaikie, the Aberdeen plumber and brassfounder. 'He walked about with much confidence, conversed freely with any officer who happened to be on deck, and generally made use of their arm to prevent his stumbling from the motion of the ship.'

On retirement from the Royal Navy, Dr Blaikie held his surgeries at his Castle Terrace house so it seemed an appropriate location for Aberdeen's first Sick Children's Hospital, within easy reach of medical classes at Marischal College, the Dispensary, and Maternity Hospital in Barnett's Close in the Guestrow, and the Royal Infirmary at Woolmanhill. It opened in 1877, the brainchild of William Stephenson Professor of Midwifery. With children

*The Royal Aberdeen Hospital for Sick Children at Castle Terrace,
formerly Dr Blaikie's townhouse. Corner balconies were added where beds
could be wheeled out into the fresh air.*

prone to so many contagious diseases, often fatal, the hospital was always full, even after it was extended and after the neighbouring house of Dr Alexander Henderson was purchased.

A little way down the road, the Castle Brae Chapel of 1865, built by John Gordon of Parkhill, founder of the Gordon Evangelical Mission, proclaimed its ecumenicism with the words 'Jesus Only', inscribed on a lintel above the door. That name attached itself both to the chapel and to its later existence as the out-patient department of the hospital. Within a few years, and with the catchment area now extending to Shetland, the Castle Terrace buildings could cope no longer and in 1929 the hospital moved to modern, spacious premises at Foresterhill. Here the city's third Sick Children's Hospital, a state-of-the-art, multi-million pound successor to Nos 6–8 Castle Terrace opened in 2003.

In 1938 Alec Hunter, the second of three generations of 'Cocky' Hunters, the famous Aberdeen institution of antique and second-hand furniture dealers, took over the old hospital building. For years a cornucopia of second-hand goods spilling out at the front of the building was a familiar scene. 'Jesus Only' became the Scandanavian Church and the flag of Sweden fluttered proudly above Virginia Street for some years. In 1972 the former hospital-cum-Cocky Hunter's and the old 'Jesus Only' building, now disused, were bought by a firm of property developers and demolished three years later. Years passed and nothing happened in Castle Terrace. It was not until the late 1980s that the site was redeveloped by another firm.

The rear of the hospital from Virginia Street with the 'Jesus Only'
out-patients' department, right.

EAST END:
THE CASTLEHILL

THE RECORDS OFFICE AND ITS NEIGHBOURS
*

We can turn now to the east end of the Castlegate where, before the Salvation Army Citadel took over, there was a little terrace of buildings. The most northerly of the row, No. 3, was the two-storey Records Office dating from 1779, custom-built to house the public records of city and county. Robert Adam, who submitted a design in 1772, may have been the architect. It had a hipped roof and a balustrade at the eaves with the central three bays advanced and pedimented, echoing the new tolbooth entrance. The historian William Kennedy condemned it as 'a plain building, devoid of ornament, and very ill-constructed'. Its dampness was apparently causing damage to valuable papers.

The sheriff clerk's department was on the ground floor, while the upper was used as the small debt court and for meetings of the county gentry. It also housed the library of the Society of Advocates in Aberdeen until the Society's own hall was built at the Back Wynd/Union Street corner in 1838. In 1833 the sheriff clerk's department and the county records were transferred to a new

The east end of the Castlegate prior to the building of the Citadel with the Records Office, left, and the townhouse of Francis Gordon.

building in King Street, and the Records Office building had to look for new custom. The following year it found itself home to Sringthorpe's Waxworks and to the city's General Dispensary, Vaccine and Lying-in Institution (Maternity Hospital), founded in 1823 for poor folk not ill enough to be admitted to hospital. The Dispensary had a tendency to rove around the east end. The Old Records Office was used both as the Burgh Police Court and as a prison while the new Town House was being built, from 1867. It was demolished in 1891 to allow for the widening of Justice Street.

The elegant, tall house with the dressed granite frontage next door, No. 5 Castle Street, was built in the early nineteenth century by Mr Francis Gordon, laird of Kincardine O'Neil as his townhouse. At the end of the row and nearly always out of the picture was a small house, the home of Dr William Brown, Principal of Marischal College and later of the well-known artist James Cassie RSA. Both houses were demolished to make way for the building of the Salvation Army Citadel, 1893–6 by James Souttar, architect.

The view of the Castlegate c. 1810, looking west by George Moir, advocate

This sketch shows the old Records Office is 'To Let', presumably between its stints as waxworks and prison. The ground floor of Mr Francis Gordon's townhouse next door is occupied by James Gordon, silk mercer. Gordon's shop was so brightly lit up with new-fangled gas that it illuminated the whole Castlegate

and Professor of Belles Lettres at Edinburgh University, was drawn from a window in Principal William Brown's house. Not artificially thronged with notables who might buy a print, the drawing is pleasing in its simplicity, with women taking buckets to the Mannie Well (not shown), shore porters carrying a sedan chair, a boy with a hoop and a man with a wheelbarrow. Three tiny figures are chatting at the entrance to Huxter Row to the left of the Town House. (Huxter Row was the traditional demarcation line between Castle Street and Union Street). The next gap to the left, with the horse and cart in front of it, is the entrance to Broad Street. To the extreme left, clothes are drying on a line at the corner leading to the site of the Futty Port and Castle Terrace, and in front of it is the side of the shop of the merchant George Stratton, nicknamed, to his annoyance, Hoggie Geordie.

The raconteur William Buchanan tells of how one evening Hoggie was annoyed by a drunken soldier returning to Castlehill Barracks who entered his shop and, addressing him by his hated nickname, requested a nightcap. Hoggie seized a bottle of ink, the nearest thing to hand, to hurl at him. The

Moir's View of the Castlegate, c. 1810

soldier fled towards Peacock's Close on the north side, Hoggie in hot pursuit.
He let the bottle fly. It missed its target and broke against Mr Peacock's
house, newly erected and the only one at that time to have a fine granite-
dressed front. It left 'a great, black, ill-looking splash'. Peacock, presumably
now dancing with rage, sued Geordie and, concludes Buchanan, 'the consequence was that Geordie had to pay a mason to restore it to its former
appearance'.

THE CASTLE

*

Behind the Records Office and its neighbours lay the Castlehill, once the site
of the enigmatic Castle of Aberdeen to which the Castlegate, the *vicus castri*,
first recorded in 1107, led in early times. This castle is thought originally to
have been a wooden motte and bailey two-fort affair, using as its foundations
the Castlehill and the Heading Hill on the other side of the future Commerce
Street. It commanded the Denburn and Dee estuaries, overlooking what

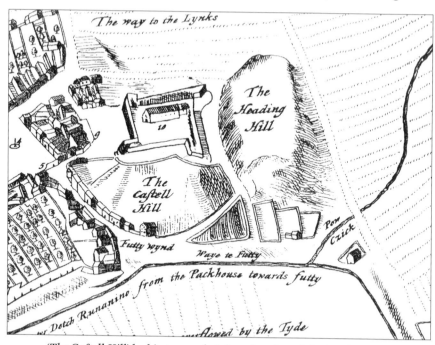

'The Caftell Hill' looking somewhat decapitated, and the Heading Hill,
shown in the detail from Parson Gordon's Plan, which may once have served as the
foundations of the shadowy motte and bailey fort. Note St Ninian's Chapel (10)
'within a New Sconce' (fortress).

Parson Gordon noted as 'The Roade', the Aberdeen roadstead or sea approaches and was protected by a difficult approach up the Shiprow and Exchequer Row. In 1264 Aberdeen's first recorded provost, Richard Cementarius (Richard the Mason), was working at the castle, perhaps reinforcing the palisades with stone against English attack.

There is an apocryphal tale that after Robert the Bruce's victory at Barra in May 1308, the triumphant Aberdeen contingent returned to the town and, buoyed with success, slaughtered the English garrison holding the castle and razed it to the ground to the battle cry of 'Bon Accord' which became the city motto. Another tale is that it was reduced in height on the instructions of Robert the Bruce to forestall reinvestment by the enemy. But there is a writ of Edward II that is fact, not legend. Issued from Windsor on 10 July 1308, it appointed William le Betour captain of his Navy, enjoining him to assist in raising the siege 'of our castle of Aberdeen and to take strong measures ... against our hostile and rebellious Scots'. After that the Castle of Aberdeen vanishes from the records without leaving any pictorial evidence of its existence.

St Ninian's Chapel

✻

St Ninian's Chapel was built within the curtilage of the old castle and endowed by the open-handed Provost Robert Blinseile in 1504 with the revenues of his property in the Shiprow. After the Reformation of 1560 this now ecclesiastically redundant building enjoyed a versatile career. In 1566, it was converted into a lighthouse with 'three great lights' shining forth between September and March, paid for by levies on harbour users. It housed the St Nicholas Kirk Sang School for several years from 1594, the choristers having been dislodged from their school in the kirkyard when the Westerkirkgate (Back Wynd) was being laid out. St Ninian's served as the commissary court for a time and it was used for the lying-in-state of the great and the good. This caught on and it became popular, in spite of a fee of ten merks (a merk being 13s 4d Scots) as an early funeral parlour where country folk could forgather prior to an interment. It later served as a gunpowder magazine and as a Quaker prison.

During Cromwell's administration of Scotland, his troops invested the Castlehill with a fort, built round St Ninian's Chapel. Masonry was scarce in the burgh, so the soldiers helped themselves to stones from the ruinous Bishop's Palace and a Chanonry manse in Old Aberdeen. Worse still, they removed the walls of the choir of St Machar's Cathedral, undermining the central tower, which resulted in its fall in 1688. Doubtless some of these stones live on in the surviving south-east bastion of the Cromwellian fort.

St Ninian's Chapel was demolished in 1794. The French Revolution was underway, unrest was in the air and the town council gifted the government all the ground within St Ninian's ramparts including the chapel, for the building of a barracks to relieve Aberdonians of the enforced and 'grievous burden' of quartering soldiers.

CASTLEHILL BARRACKS

*

The barracks was a handsome building of three storeys and a basement, in granite ashlar, costing £16,000. The parade ground was laid out over the site of St Ninian's Chapel. The barracks dominated the Castlehill for over a hundred years before being hidden from view by the Salvation Army Citadel. The Argyllshire Fencibles was the first regiment to be quartered there, in November 1794, and thereafter, for almost a century and a half, the barracks was the scene of frequent comings and goings by all the Scottish Regiments

The main block of the imposing Castlehill Barracks, embellished by a central pediment, ran east to west while two south-facing ranges at either end looked across to the harbour.

and some Irish. During the nineteenth century there were spats, some of a serious nature, between the soldiery and the citizenry in the Castlegate area; the Connaught Rangers was the regiment most often in trouble. The presence of the soldiers brought prostitutes flocking to the area and this, coupled with the move west of the respectable merchant classes, left the Castlegate in the nineteenth century with an unenviable reputation for vice and drunkenness.

On 15 August 1935, to the skirl of pipes, the Gordon Highlanders marched smartly out of the Castlehill Barracks for the last time and up King Street to their new barracks at the Bridge of Don. Two months later the first families from the former Jute Works in Froghall moved in. Castlehill Barracks had been designated a 'transfer housing colony' for families made homeless by slum clearance. Tenants who 'proved satisfactory' over a period of time got on to the council housing list, but many folk found it not too bad a place to live. Castlehill Barracks could have been handsomely restored, like Richards Ltd's old warehouse, now 'The Bastille', but it was demolished in 1965. In 1971, as the architect-historian Edward Meldrum put it in *Aberdeen of Old*, 'this historic site was built over with flats of a mediocre design unfitting in such an important setting'.

THE NORTH SIDE

We can turn now to the north side of the Castlegate. It has been dominated by the edifices of local government and justice since that day in 1407 when, in implementation of a charter of 1394 of King Robert III, every man in Aberdeen was instructed to give a day's labour or pay four pence towards the construction of a tolbooth (originally, a booth where the citizenry paid tolls or dues). The charter permitted its erection anywhere you please (*ubicunque*) in the burgh except the centre of the market place. The ensuing, if tardy tolbooth, was built remarkably near the forbidden territory, if the site of its seventeenth-century stone successor, by Thomas Watson of Old Rayne, is anything to go by.

Overleaf the high tolbooth or jail is the tower-house with spire at the east end; the laich or low tolbooth adjoins it to the west. Here the town council met, the law courts convened and the city's ammunition was stored. The long row of houses behind was Huxter Row, which ran nearly as far east as the present King Street. The premises of Edward Raban, Aberdeen's first printer, and his successors, were thereabouts and from there too came the first issue of the *Aberdeen Journal*, printed in 1746 by James Chalmers. Robert

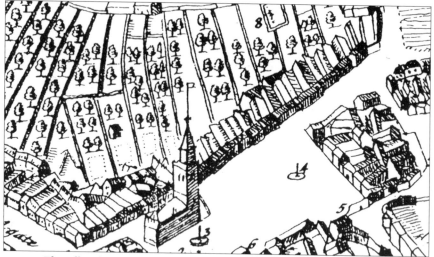

The tolbooth in the Castlegate, behind the Market Cross (3), predecessor
of the present Cross. Huxter Row runs behind. Detail from Parson Gordon.

Gordon, founder of the College that bears his name, was born in Huxter Row
in 1668. Parson Gordon, Robert Gordon's uncle as it happens, shows a gap to
the left of the laich tolbooth. This was a shortcut leading from the south side
of the Castlegate into Huxter Row. One could then turn left to walk through
the short 'rump' of the Row into the Broadgate, extreme left.

The high tolbooth had four vaults over each other with a platform roof
and battlement and was built between 1616 and 1622, with the spire added in
1629. There were later replacements. Its formidable appearance was deceptive. It was notorious for the number of escapes successfully carried out by
its clientele. In March 1673, for example, Lord Frendraught, Francis Irvine of
Hilton and James Gordon:

> broke from the upper part of the Tolbuith, wherin they wer, and
> made a holl, by taking out certain of the keystones thereof, and came
> down to the Laich Tolbuith by ane tow, and broke open the eistmost
> dore of the tolbuith and escaped.

The easternmost door was the only way in or out. Piecemeal improvements
took place down the years, particularly from 1729 when William Adam
created a three-storey building out of the old, with council chamber and
courtrooms. A major refurbishment followed in 1750 when a new town hall
was built over the courtroom, specifically for council meetings, a high-roofed,
elegant room with a chimney-piece of variegated marble from Holland and

finely cut crystal chandeliers of Belgian origin with twelve crystal sconces (candlesticks) on the side walls. The frontage was standardised at this time, designed and constructed by Patrick Barron, wright, a stalwart of the Seven Incorporated Trades and owner of the Woodside estate. On a thrifty note, the cost was to be not more than 300 guineas and the ground floor was to be rented out to shops, though butchers weren't welcome.

The New Inn and the Mason Lodge

*

Since 1670 the Aberdeen Lodge of Freemasons had held their meetings at Futty's Mire on the Links, but in 1755 the magistrate feued them the vacant ground immediately east of the tolbooth 'as a lodge or place of meeting'. Access in those days was by a new road, laid out by the masons, Lodge Walk,

This detail from Seaton's View of the Castlegate, 1806, shows The New Inn left of the Market Cross. The tolbooth and its double staircase are extreme left. Several shops tenanted the ground floor including the State Lottery Office, with a customer entering. The Records Office and Mr Brown's townhouse are at the east end. The tall man, right, with two elegantly dressed ladies is Seaton's patron, the Castlegate merchant, John Ewen. The hangman, John Milne foreground is selecting fish from a creel, one of the 'perks' of his job.

via North Street and past the Flesh Market. The Mason Lodge itself took up only one room in the upper storey while the rest of the building was to be an 'Inn or Tavern for the accommodation of Inhabitants and strangers for this now populous [15,730 in 1755] and flourishing city'. The magistrates had given the masons every encouragement, for 'this was an undertaking much wanted'. (Skipper Scott's Tavern nearby was out of action, Francis Peacock having acquired it for his dancing classes.) The New Inn was designed to match the three-storey townhouse which it adjoined, blending uniformity and architectural good taste. However it obliterated the townhouse's easternmost and only door, so a double staircase was built, with a pedimented porch giving access to the first floor of the tolbooth and so to the Town House.

DISTINGUISHED VISITORS

*

The Mason Lodge was dedicated in January 1757 while the New Inn quickly established itself as the town's leading hostelry. Mrs McGhie, the first land-lady, almost missed the privilege of welcoming Dr Johnson and Boswell when they stayed in Aberdeen on 21 August 1773 en route to the Western Isles. The

Left, The New Inn and the Mason Lodge with its gable-end Venetian window and three windows facing the Castlegate. (Hugh Irvine). The Inn and the houses, extreme right, were replaced by the North Bank. Right, Lodge Walk accessed the Lodge from the rear. The pend, centre, leads into the Castlegate. The tolbooth spire dominates both pictures. (I.W. Davidson).

inn was full. Fortunately an old waiter recalled Boswell's father, the judge Lord Auchinleck, who lodged there while on circuit, and a room was found. (Auchinleck had wittily nicknamed the bear-like Dr Johnson 'Ursa Major', the Great Bear). George Smith succeeded Mrs McGhie as landlord. He had 'an interest in the Edinburgh fly' and developed the inn as a coaching establishment with stabling for sixty horses and twelve pairs for posting. He also invested in a new hearse which 'will go to any part of the country and sufficient post chaises to attend if required'.

Peter Wilkie took over from George Smith and on 10 September 1787 welcomed 'Mr Burns, the celebrated Ayrshire bard' on the latter's memorable visit to Aberdeen during his Highland tour. Wilkie who had recently put in a new public room, could offer twenty-four parlours, a coffee room, a drawing room for balls and assemblies, and stabling for thirty-six horses with 'commodious haylofts and granaries'. Burns may have been impressed but he left no record of it. He scrambled up the 'long and rather steep outer stair' to Chalmers' printing office, now based in an old silk mill behind the townhouse, presumably in Huxter Row, for a chat with the printer and other local literati including John Skinner, Episcoplian Bishop of Aberdeen and son of James Skinner, whose poem 'Tullochgorum' Burns admired above all others.

HUXTER ROW
*

Huxter Row is first mentioned in 1440 as the Boothrawe, a row of booths or little shops. Then it became Huckster Wynd, a huckster being a packman, an itinerant salesman. It is unclear how the 'rawe' functioned. Did the hucksters open their booths every day? Or only on market days? What did they sell? Perhaps John Ewen started off there.

THE LEMON TREE
*

By the time Burns visited Aberdeen in 1787 Huxter Row was best known as home to several of the city's taverns, the most famous being the Lemon Tree. It was the favoured meeting place of Aberdeen's café society, a convivial but respectable gathering of academics, scribes, ministers, booksellers and magistrates. The Aberdeen Philosophical or Wise Club, founded in 1758, met there and Professor James Beattie, the most famous man in the kingdom following the publication of his poem 'The Minstrel' (1771–4) was a patron. The inn features in Neil Maclean's *Life at a Northern University* as the 'Café Royal' where a room was specially set apart for students. In one of the most notorious episodes in the book the classmates carouse there with sundry tumblers of toddy then set out for Old Aberdeen, where they remove the wheels from a cart and get involved in a punch-up with locals. The inn features under its own name in William Alexander's classic, *Johnny Gibb of Gushetneuk*, where Mains of Yawall and the Rev. Andew Sleekaboot come to town via the Aberdeenshire Canal's gig boat and put up at 'that well respected hostelry, the Lemon Tree'. Sleekaboot was by no means the only cleric to frequent the place. It was a favourite of the Aberdeen ministers who assembled there after a Synod meeting:

> *And now methinks at four I see*
> *The brethren all in Lemon Tree*
> *For here they fail not to convene*
> *Round Ronald's smoking hot tureen*

George Ronald was landlord from 1799 and his widow carried on after his death in 1819 until her retirement in 1859. There was a long tradition of good food. Even before the Ronalds' time the shore porters would repair there for 'a sumptuous meal of pease soup followed by a fricassee of chicken or a saddle of roast mutton, topped by a pudding of milk and rice or an apple tart', for as little as two pence sterling a head. William Carnie, who met there weekly with his cronies, immortalises Mrs Ronald in *Reporting Reminiscences* (Vol. 1, 1902). 'There never was such creamy Finnan haddocks, such magnificent partin claws as Mrs Ronald was wont to place on the table ...' On her retirement after sixty years in the trade Carnie recalled how the Dean of Guild led her in, 'dressed in her best and amplest black silk gown, the snow-white set-up cap, handbag over the arm'. Then 'old couthie, courteous Mrs Ronald' was toasted by 'a goodly party of sixty citizens'.

THE END OF HUXTER ROW
*

It was the end of an era. Between 1818–20 John Smith, the city architect, drew up plans for a new courthouse behind the townhouse and behind that, a new jail, the East Prison. A watch-house or police station was provided in Huxter Row, at the rear of the courthouse, almost next door to the Lemon Tree. The part of Huxter Row buildings that ran behind the tolbooth was demolished.

It was at this time too that the double stairs and porch outside the tolbooth were removed.

There had also been a major change down at the New Inn end, which not only removed any surviving remnants of the east end of Huxter Row, but also the New Inn itself. Plans to build a modern hotel on the New Inn's site, drawn up by Isaac Machray, coaching supremo and landlord of the Royal Hotel across in Union Street, were scuppered in 1838 when the directors of the North of Scotland Bank led by the formidable Alexander Anderson, who would be Lord Provost from 1859–65, stepped in and purchased and demolished the New Inn and adjacent buildings on King Street, to make way for the North Bank's Head Office. Archibald Simpson was chosen as architect, though his tender of £7,200 was the highest. The foundation stone was laid in January 1840 and, owing to the unavoidable absence of the New Inn, the company then crossed to the Royal Hotel for a nosh-up. (The Royal Hotel survives. It was later remodelled as Falconers department store and subsequently Frasers which closed down at the end of 2002.) 'The contractors were

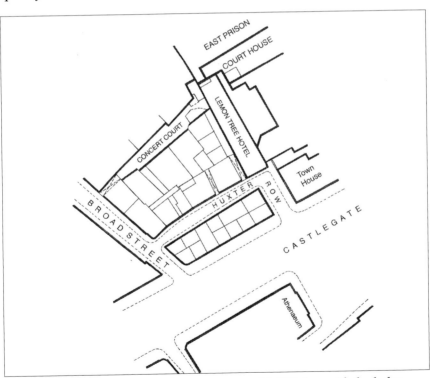

By 1820 all that remained of Huxter Row was this little lane with the dogleg between the townhouse and Broad Street. Entrance to the Row from Castle Street was opposite the end of the Athenaeum.

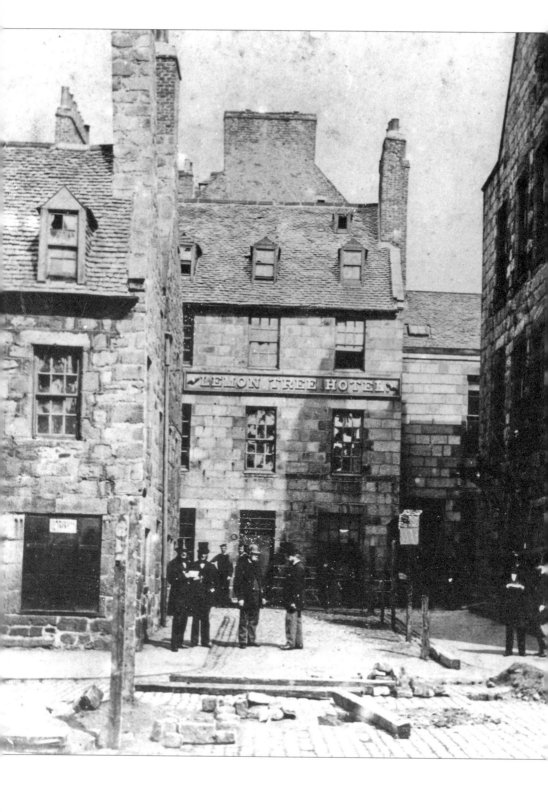

all Aberdeen tradesmen', wrote Alexander Keith, and 'the solid and majestic new building as it rose above the narrow-shouldered houses of the Castlegate caused a sensation.' Completed in 1842, the magnificent North Bank represented a new triumphalist mode in Aberdeen's architectural styles. (It became the Clydesdale and North after amalgamation and is now a pub.)

The rump of Huxter Row survived for another quarter of a century. Its residents included policemen, court officials, shopkeepers and civil servants as well as publicans. Peter Machray took over at the Lemon Tree on Mrs Ronald's retirement, followed by his widow, who received notice to quit in 1867: what remained of Huxter Row was due to be demolished to make way for the new municipal buildings. The inn transferred its picturesque name to St Nicholas Street, to premises later much altered and occupied for many years by Claude Alexander, then Richard Shops. William Coull took over the Lemon Tree Mark II in 1911, but by 1935 had acquired the Prince of Wales round the corner in St Nicholas Lane. The Lemon Tree closed for good, though much later a popular entertainment venue took over the name.

Garey's photograph, overleaf, was taken in the nick of time. Dr Johnson's comment of a hundred years earlier, 'Aberdeen has all the bustle of a prosperous trade and all the show of increasing opulence,' remained true. Civic headquarters worthy of city and county, reflecting growth and affluence, were overdue. All the buildings in Garey's photograph west of the tolbooth and round into Broad Street as far north as Concert Court, were swept away and replaced between 1867–73 by the then municipal and county buildings, today's Town House and sheriff court complex. The tolbooth remains incorporated within the building, the spire still rises above Lodge Walk and the 1816 clock 'of superior workmanship' by John Gartly, the Exchequer Row watchmaker, still keeps the time. But Peddie & Kinnear, the Edinburgh-based architects of the complex, also paid subtle homage to the city's architectural past. Arcading, such a notable feature of older Aberdeen buildings,

Left.
The gentlemen outside the Lemon Tree in 1867 are not waiting for the pub to open but are senior members of the police force from the Huxter Row watch-house nearby, keeping the photographer under surveillance. By the 1860s the upper echelons of the Aberdeen force boasted a superintendent, two lieutenants, seven sergeants and two detectives, several of whom are pictured here. Broken window panes and debris in the street indicate, not criminal damage, but demolition to make way for the present municipal buildings. Right, the building at the edge of Castle Street is the west corner of the Town House. The wide gap is the south–north section of Huxter Row. Left, the start of Union Street, with James Macdonald's tobacconist's shop extreme left.

is echoed and even the little garret dormer windows of the past have been acknowledged and ennobled with tiny, steeply pitched roofs. During his visit in the 1840s the artist R.W. Billings had written:

> Aberdeen is remarkable for the number of private dwellings orna-
> mented by that light, graceful singular turret which was adapted
> from French chateau architecture; they are a striking and lasting
> memorial of the extent, which, before the Union of the Crowns the
> habits and ideas of our Continental allies were finding their way
> into the most distant parts of Scotland.

Peddie & Kinnear decided that the day of the turret was not yet over. They ran riot and embellished the new Town House in a glorious rash of fairytale towers. Just as well, for none of the originals remain.

William Garey's photograph of 1867 gives an extended perspective of the area shown on page 60. From right in Castle Street: the North Bank (the splendid entrance, on the corner with King Street is out of sight), the tolbooth with tower and spire, the Town House with two shops on the ground floor, William Smith, tobacconists with awnings, and A. Smith, outfitters. Next, the entry to Huxter Row, then Nos 6–18 Union Street. The low building is James McDonald tobacconist, then a bootmaker, the Valuations Office, an outfitter, a bookseller, another bootmaker and Chapman & Co. tailors and clothiers, extreme left, whose building continued round into Broad Street. The shops were entered from Union Street, the houses above from Huxter Row.

CHAPTER 3

THE BROADGATE
AND THE GALLOWGATE

BROAD STREET

EAST SIDE

*

The Broadgate, or Broad Street as it became as early as the eighteenth century, and the Gallowgate, the route out of town for those travelling north, were really the same street, though Broad Street was a continuation of the Gallowgate rather than the other way around. At the point where the Gallowgate broadened out it became the Broadgate of the Gallowgate, then just the Broadgate. The area around has a rich archaeological heritage and was settled in part in the late thirteenth century. Broad Street, even during

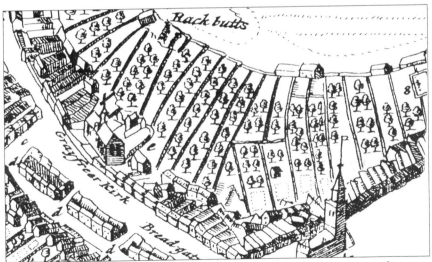

The east side of Parson Gordon's Broadgate shows about a dozen two-storey houses and a handful of backhouses, with long rigs running to the Backbuts, later (West) North Street. Moving north there are about half-a-dozen single-storey houses, then Greyfriars Kirk with spire with the little buildings of Marischal College (e) alongside.

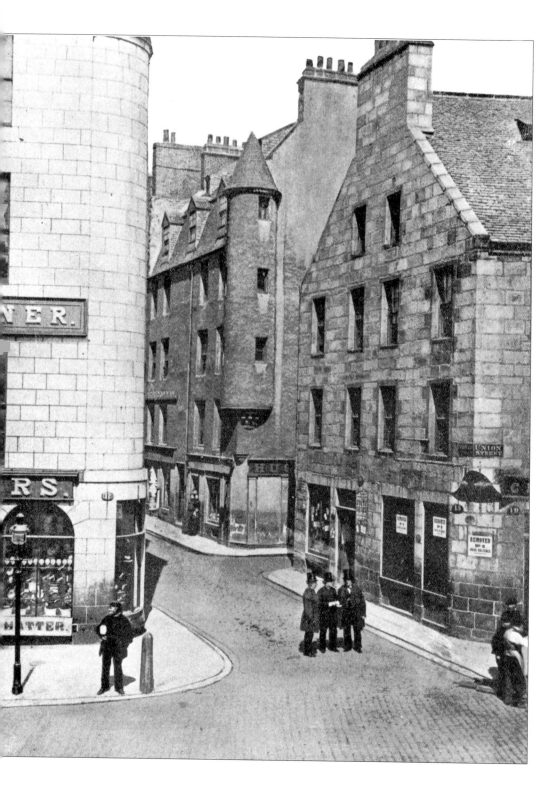

the twentieth century, has been altered beyond recognition. There were several distinct phases of 'dinging doon', the first in 1867.

Nos 2–10 Broad Street
*

The three groups of buildings in this photograph by Johnston Shearer show interesting contrasts in style. The building of white, dressed granite left, forming a curved corner to Union Street was at that time occupied by Messrs Steele & Co, hatters on the corner and Mr Henderson, stationer and bookbinder on the first floor. It was later owned by Esslemont & Macintosh. The building extreme right, whose gable-end turns the corner from Union Street into Broad Street is that of Chapman & Co., clothiers, the last in that row of shops, Nos 6–18 Union Street, west of the old Town House already discussed. The shop at the gable-end next to Chapman & Co. belonged to the bookseller, George Shepherd. Huxter Row emerges into Broad Street between the gable-end and the turreted house which was the scene of an exchange between Dr Samuel Johnson (in Aberdeen with Boswell in 1773) and a workman carrying out some harling. Johnson courteously hoped that he was not getting in the way. 'Na, na,' replied the workman in true nippy Aberdeen fashion, dashing a trowelful of lime against the wall. 'Yer nae in my wye if yer nae in yer ain.' We do not know the response of 'Ursa Major'. The last shop in the photograph was owned by James Connon, draper. Only the chimneystack of the next building appears, belonging to Anderson & Thomson, clothiers. The number of clothiers, drapers and tailors in Aberdeen in the eighteenth and nineteenth centuries seems to have been extraordinarily large.

This little group of buildings is not within living memory; it was demolished and replaced by the west wall of the townhouse at the Broad Street corner (with the clock in the wall) going as far back as Concert Court. The municipal buildings were set further back than the line of these old houses. The pepperpot turret was the sole survivor, rescued by the convener of the county, Mr A.F. Irvine of Drum.

Left.
Broad Street at its junction with Union Street, prior to 1867 when demolition to clear the site for the present municipal buildings started. The three men at the mouth of Broad Street were Baillie Hugh Ross, left, a town councillor whose business was on the ground floor of the tall, seventeenth-century house with pepperbox turret. William Forsyth, editor of the Aberdeen Journal, *centre is taking notes, and Councillor George Jamieson, of Jamieson's Quay fame, provost from 1874–80, is right.*

CONCERT COURT
*

Next to Anderson & Thompson, out of the picture and almost backing on to the north end of the Lemon Tree, was Concert Court, a narrow close entered by a pend. There were a number of buildings and houses on either side, including an Episcopalian meeting house which was set on fire and gutted during the persecutions of 1746. On a happier note, weekly concerts of the Musical Society, hence the name, were held there from 1748–1838. John Ross, organist of St Paul's Chapel in the Gallowgate, organised concerts, dancing master Francis Peacock performed on the violin and violoncello and John Ewen of Castlegate fame was treasurer for many years. Concert Court is the only Broad Street court to survive the various demolitions and though not lost, was opened up, widened, hedged by municipal offices and became the access to the newly built handsome headquarters of the Society of Advocates who moved from their Union Street-Back Wynd headquarters to link up with the new sheriff court.

NOS 12–34 BROAD STREET
*

Five courts, picking up from Concert (extreme right, and out of picture again), punctuated this section of Broad Street: Well, Cruden's, Rettie's and Chronicle. All are gone now. On the extreme right are an outfitters and a servants' registry, which were there for years. The central building with the light fascia, concealing the granite arches of the arcaded windows, was the home of Aberdeen Journals from 1894, with its rolls of newsprint, distinctive smell and labyrinthine corridors. The works entrance through Cruden's Court, to the left, was shared with families in the tenements above. The buildings, originally owned by Bailie William Cruden, stretched back to the East Prison. The bailie's son Alexander 'the Corrector' was born there in 1700, 'a Protestant, a fanatic and more than a little mad'. He was the author of a famous *Concordance to the Bible*. At least two rooms dating from Baillie Cruden's time were still intact in 1970 when Aberdeen Journals departed to Mastrick. Beyond Cruden's Court was Charles Coutts, a chemist, at No. 26 with Rettie's Court behind. Middleton Rettie, a tinsmith, held property there at the beginning of the nineteenth century. The Northern Loan Company (we are in three balls territory) at No. 32, and Ewen & Co, cabinetmakers, at No. 34, on the corner with Queen Street, were long-time occupants. Between them, Chronicle Court ran along the backs of the Queen Street houses, giving access to the rear of No. 10 Queen Street.

Nos 12–34 Broad Street. This terrace of tall granite-fronted buildings dating from the late seventeenth to the early nineteenth centuries was demolished in 1973 to make way for a tiled extension to the Town House. Marischal College is extreme left.

By 1970 Aberdeen Journals decided to relocate from their antiquated and cramped premises and sold the building to Aberdeen Town Council, who demolished this entire section of Broad Street in 1973 to make way for an extension to the Town House. The lost houses, though shabby and worn, had style and dignity. With the arcading reinstated, fenestration made uniform, interiors gutted and frontages restored, an imaginative wing to the Town House might have been created. However, a modern extension in ceramic tiling had replaced the old houses by 1975, even extending across Concert Court.*

* Tiled extensions have their drawbacks. Soon after this block was completed a bus drew up outside and what appeared to be men on an outing tumbled out and dashed inside. Watchers across in St Nicholas House were puzzling over what type of civic reception the busload were attending when the men re-emerged looking sheepish and were driven round to the Upperkirkgate, where they presumably found what they were looking for.

QUEEN STREET:
SHOPS, INNS AND OFFICES
*

In the plan at the start of this chapter, Parson Gordon shows us the line of the Broadgate running unbroken from the Castlegate to the Gallowgate, but that all changed in 1775 when the house of Andrew Thomson of Crawton, an advocate, was demolished and a new street laid out through its grounds. The purpose was to provide easy access for those living in the Broadgate, the Guestrow and the west side of town to the Flesh and Meal Markets that had been set up near Lodge Walk. 'We hear that the elegant new street leading from the Broadgate to the Meal Market is named Queen Street in honour of

Left. No. 10 Queen Street, where the Byron family lived. It was a three-storey house of plain coursed granite, with a little window in the central gablet. The round-arched pend, right, gave access to Chronicle Court, which led through to Broad Street.

Right. A shop and house at the east end of Queen Street, at the junction with West North Street, with steeply pitched roof and arcading at the ground floor.

our gracious sovereign [Queen Charlotte],' reported the *Aberdeen Journal* on 4 November 1776.

During 1790–1, the two-year-old George Gordon, the future Lord Byron, and his mother Catherine lived at No. 10, on the south side over the shop of their landlord, James Anderson, a family friend, who witnessed various deeds for the Byron family. The name Bryon was unknown in Aberdeen and usually misspelt, so Catherine used her maiden name, the most important one in the north-east, as her surname, and was known as Mrs Byron Gordon. Anderson was a fancy goods merchant and presided over an Aladdin's Cave of perfumes, pearl pins, earrings, necklaces, shoe and knee-buckles, watches, fancy feathers, gloves, silk umbrellas, spangles, fans, snuff boxes, military hats, men's round hats, ladies' beaver hats and fancy hats for children. He also ran a ticket agency for the seasonal theatres in town, including the Queen Street Theatre, as did Mr Morrison of the Queen Street hat manufactory, perhaps one of his suppliers. Byron's mother would also have appreciated James Clunes' shop nearby, which sold super-fine muffnets, rich black armozeen (taffeta), black lutestring (a rich satin), broad and narrow modes, satin coats, marfielled bed covers and counterpanes.

Some of the houses on the north side in Byron's time stood in an acre of ground and stretched back to Shoe Lane, laid out at much the same time by the Shoemaker Craft of the Incorporated Trades. The Society of Golfers would meet at Masson's Inn for dinner at 4 o'clock. It boasted 'a complete set of stables' and 'an elegant hall'. James Staats Forbes, Queen Street's (and indeed Aberdeen's) leading entrepreneur, property developer and grocer, sold luxury goods at his licensed 'delicatessen' on the north side including 'new' teas, coffee, chocolate, 'spiceries', figs, raisins, Jamaica rum and cognac. 'Staats' was much involved with laying out the Lochlands of which George Street would be the main street. Plans of this new development could be viewed at his shop-cum-office. Nos 39–43, a three-storey L-plan building dating from 1776, was built by John Farquhar and the local architect William Littlejohn. They added the Queen Street Theatre at the back in the 1780s. On the second floor was the meeting hall of the St Machar Freemasons' lodge. It became the Aberdeen Hotel around 1790, then the Oddfellows Hall, after being acquired by that society. It was demolished in 1969. John Mitchell, Chartist leader and a poet of 'fiery rhapsodies', opened a bookshop in Queen Street, where he edited the short-lived *Aberdeen Review*, around 1830. Here too, John Smith, who with Archibald Simpson was one of the architects of the Granite City, had his office in the first half of the nineteenth century.

By the late nineteenth century, Richard Smith, leather merchant and

When John Smith designed the North Parish Church in 1830 (today the Aberdeen Arts Centre), it was as a powerful yet elegant hinge that linked King Street (left, 1803) and Queen Street (right, 1776). Smith later lived and worked at No. 142 King Street and would have viewed his old Queen Street office and splendid church every time he rode into Aberdeen.

boot-top manufacturer; William Rattray, tobacco and snuff manufacturer; and William Green, wholesale grocer, were all prominent enough to go into the industrial digest *Scotland of Today*, as was John Mason and Son, plain and decorative painters, who had an extensive business at Nos 34–8 for about eighty years from 1866. They made stained-glass windows for numerous churches including Queen's Cross and provided the décor for 'many private mansions in Aberdeen'. Within living memory, on the left-hand side were Gray Watt & Co, long-established hardware merchants, and Neil & Co, the music shop beside Shoe Lane, with Robert Ogilvie's wholesale warehouse and showroom next to it. On the right-hand side were Ewen's furniture shop which turned the corner from Broad Street and the Northern Loan Co., pawnbrokers. John Dean, plumber and electrician, was at No. 32 from 1883, specialising in installing servants' bell-boards among other things. At Nos 50–4 were Edmond & Spark, bookbinders and publishers, where as students we would go to buy notebooks wholesale. Beyond Lodge Walk at No. 66 was the man himself, baker and hot rowie specialist Sir Thomas Mitchell, the shrewd, pawky and well-loved lord provost of Aberdeen from 1938–47. This Georgian street may have become drab and dingy, but restoration would have been worthwhile. John Dean the plumber was still there in 1973, when the entire street was pulled down and the firm celebrated its centenary elsewhere.

LONGACRE

*

Longacre, a narrow street with a curiously un-Aberdeen name, ran parallel to Queen Street (which it pre-dated) and Marischal College. The entry from Broad Street was by a pend. John Smith, the architect, began his married life there, handily placed for his office in Queen Street. Here was the house of Bishop Skinner, whom Burns would meet during his visit to Aberdeen in 1787. The Scottish Episcopalians were established in Aberdeen in 1715, first, disastrously, in Concert Court, then in the Guestrow and by the late 1770s in Longacre. Bishop Skinner fitted up the upper floors as a chapel and kept the lower floor as the family home. There, in the upper room at Longacre, on 14 November 1784, Skinner and two colleagues, by the laying on of hands, conse-

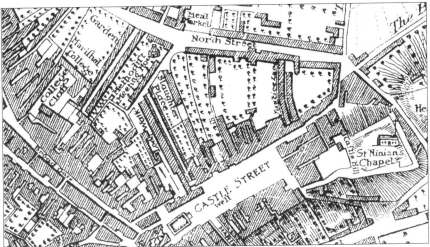

Above Castle Street (the Castlegate), Lodge Walk and 'Slaughter Place' (which was beside the Flesh Market) can be made out. The octagonal Methodist Meeting House, where Wesley himself enjoyed preaching, was in the line of the future Queen Street. The Methodists later moved to Longacre and the Free North Kirk was built on the site of the Meeting House. Longacre, unnamed and entered from North Street, runs straight between the Marischal College Garden and the Methodist Meeting House. Beyond Broadgate a pend led to the College Close, below which is Greyfriars Chapel. The little alley, hopefully 'dichted', can be made out. Beyond is Marischal College, at that time a towerhouse. From Taylor's Plan, 1773.

St Andrew's Episcopalian Chapel, Longacre, later the Old Wesleyan Church.

crated Samuel Seabury of Connecticut, former Edinburgh student and Yale graduate, as Bishop of the United States of America. Thus was the Episcopal Church in America established.

Bishop Skinner's congregation grew and by 1795 the Longacre house was demolished and a new chapel, St Andrew's, built in its place. Skinner and his still-increasing congregation moved again, to a new St Andrew's church in King Street in 1816, a fine building in Gothic style designed by Archibald

Longacre in the 1930s prior to demolition. It was replaced by the new south wing of Marischal College, where a plaque commemorates the consecration of Samuel Seabury.

Simpson. It was raised to cathedral status in 1914. Meanwhile the Wesleyan Methodists, settled in Aberdeen since the 1750s, bought St Andrew's Longacre, and this was the hub of their activities from 1818–73.

MARISCHAL COLLEGE:
THE GREYFRIARS MONASTERY
*

We have arrived at the north end of Broad Street, and at one of the most famous buildings in the world. To begin near the beginning, in 1471, the Franciscans or Greyfriars – or at least a 'reformed' section of them, the Observantines – were granted waste ground on the east side of the Broadgate by an Aberdeen burgess, Richard Vaus. Here they built their monastery and laid out their garden. Some fifty years later Gavin Dunbar, Bishop of Aberdeen, gifted them 1,400 merks to erect a new chapel. In 1559, shortly before the Reformation burst on Aberdeen, the Greyfriars made over their monastery to the town council and fled to Belgium. The 'rascal multitude' from the Mearns was frustrated in its attempts to 'ding doon' the monastery when the citizens arrived in force and 'hindered its ruin'.

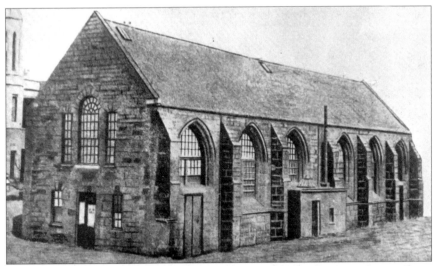

Greyfriars Kirk, funded by Bishop Gavin Dunbar, was of sandstone with a steeply pitched roof and originally, a little spire or flèche. The massive south window had seven lights and basket tracery that was unique in Scotland. On its west side deep-splayed, pointed windows were flanked by massive buttresses. It may have been Dunbar's answer to Elphinstone's masterpiece, King's College Chapel, to which it bore more than a passing resemblance. Only the crown tower was missing.

THE NEW COLLEGE

*

After the Reformation the town council rented out the Greyfriars' buildings to various tenants, but in April 1593 gave the whole monastery over to George Keith, fourth Earl Marischal (renumbered from fifth) and known to have an interest in education, to found a college. The time was right, for former church revenues were available for endowment, especially if one was favoured by the King, James VI, as Keith was. There were murmurings against the Earl's financing of his secular college with church money but his response was 'So what?' or, in the idiom of the time, 'They haf said, what say they, lat them say.' He had this scornful rejoinder engraved over the mantelpiece of his college and it survives in the current building. But King's College, founded nearly a hundred years earlier by Bishop Elphinstone, lay less than two miles away in Old Aberdeen. What had prompted this academic overkill?

The old argument that the Earl had set up Marischal College as the Protestant answer to Catholic King's College does not hold water. King's turned Protestant in 1569, nine years after the rest of Scotland it is true, but

Broad Street in the early nineteenth century with the pend leading into the college close, left, with Guild's fore-house next to it. The apartments of the young George Gordon, later Lord Byron, were next to the house with the middle turret. These houses date from the late sixteenth to the eighteenth century. Drawn by William Purser, 1833.

a quarter of a century before the Earl established his college. Protestants did not come more devout than the first post-Reformation principal at King's, the young theologian Alexander Arbuthnot, a close friend of the great Protestant reformers and a cousin, by marriage, of the Earl Marischal's sister. There were other, less high-minded, reasons. One was the Earl's rivalry with a neighbouring laird, Sir Alexander Fraser of Philorth, who established a university at Fraserburgh in 1592. Marischal College was founded a year later. Moreover, Aberdeen's magistrates had long resented the location of an establishment as prominent as King's College in the 'mere village' of Old Aberdeen, hence their eagerness to transfer the ownership of the Greyfriars' buildings to someone as prominent as the Earl, on condition that he would 'erect a philosophy college there'. Nevertheless, in its early years it was often called the New College, in deference to King's. The initial intake was six bursars and six staff, with the emphasis on teaching the philosophy of Aristotle.

When Greyfriars Kirk was built around 1520 it lay open to the street. But Aberdeen was running out of space and by 1623 substantial houses had been erected in front of kirk and college, regardless of prohibitions against shutting out natural light. Both found themselves in a gloomy courtyard, hidden from view. Worse still, there was no way in. Dr William Guild came to the rescue. That year he bought a fore-house in the Broadgate in front of Greyfriars Kirk which he gifted to the town, 'that they mack a fair and commodious entrie to the college of this burgh and to the Grayfrier Kirk'. The delighted magistrates promised to erect the entrance of ashlar work (dressed granite) and, conveniently, to build a stationer's shop beside it. This new gateway was eventually completed in 1633 and, though later enlarged, remained the only entrance to the college until 1893 when it was taken down.

GREYFRIARS CHURCH
*

Though the church was included as part of the Greyfriars' assets to be handed over to the Earl Marischal, property was swapped and the town became responsible for it. The church was neglected, 'lyen waist' and used as a bothy by soldiers and craftsmen. Before the fore-houses went up, 'all sorts of people' had access and were taking the doors and locks away, storing timber inside and using the close giving entrance to the kirk as a public toilet 'to the great dishonour of this burgh'. The council ordered that the close was to be 'cleansed and dichtit', the kirk locked up and the timber removed. Dr Guild came to the rescue once again, along with a merchant, Alexander Stewart. In 1633 they paid for glass to be installed in the windows. Commodious 'daskis' (pews) were set up and reformed services got underway for the first time.

But kirk and college were uneasy bedfellows. In 1653 the masters of Marischal set up a class for Latin improvers in the kirk, 'since there are not chalmers in the college to be spared'. The scholars were badly behaved and lessons were not resumed until they were penned into the aisle nearest the college. In 1661 the Earl Marischal, grandson of the founder, claimed Greyfriars Kirk for the private use of the college. The town council set up a watch in case the college attempted a takeover of the kirk to carry out a laureation ceremony, then protested that they had to shell out for candles, tobacco and pipes for the watchmen. The college made new keys for the kirk, refusing to hand one over to the council, who instructed the master of kirk work to put on new locks. Eventually in December 1667 the tit-for-tat-struggle was abandoned and the Earl Marischal gave up all claims to Greyfriars Kirk.

Marischal College was a plain building with two wings. A large lecture room occupied the ground floor, a public hall with heraldic ceiling the first, the library the second. Lodgings for three of the professors as well as the divinity hall and classrooms were in the wings, the addition by Adam being on the right (Delineation of Aberdeen, Robert Wilson, 1822).

THE NEW WORK
*

Meanwhile the old monastery buildings were growing increasingly damp, shabby and cramped and to compound it all, on 27 September 1639, according to the chronicler James Spalding, 'the east quarter of the Colledge Marschall suddantlie took fire'. Restoration and expansion were essential and during the later seventeenth century and the first half of the eighteenth, several fund-raising initiatives were undertaken, headed by the masters and town council, which met with excellent responses. A north wing, the 'New Work', was built and between 1737–41 further improvements were made to the ancient monastery buildings, with an extensive south wing designed by the architect William Adam being added.

Marischal College by James Skene. A corbelled-out stair turret on the north wing leads up to the observatory of 1795. The roof is guarded by a balustrade. What looks like a wind sock is a telescope. Abseiling equipment appears to be in place below! It is uncertain how the coach, if not the horses, got through the college arch.

THE MARISCHAL OBSERVATORY

✳

The teaching of astronomy began in 1690 and four years later the town council voted to give 500 merks towards 'the observatories in the New Work of the said College'. By 1781, Dr Patrick Copland, who taught natural philosophy, had erected an observatory on the Castlehill but had to dismantle it in 1795 to make way for a powder magazine for the new Castlehill Barracks. In compensation the Government funded a new observatory on the flat top of the north wing of the college and astronomical studies returned there.

THE MARISCHAL QUAD

✳

By the late eighteenth century, Marischal College buildings, including Adam's wing, were found to be 'neither regular, elegant nor commodious'. They were replaced from 1837–44, after much discussion, by a graceful and well-proportioned set of buildings to designs by Archibald Simpson. Unfortunately by then Greyfriars Kirk had been spoilt by clumsy and inappropriate alterations, its north end truncated to allow the entrance arch to be widened. However, an east aisle complete with gallery was added to accommodate the professors and students and, crammed with pews and lofts, Greyfriars at last became officially the College Kirk.

Archibald Simpson's Marischal College, built of Rubislaw granite, cost £30,000, half of which was funded by the Treasury.

THE BROAD STREET FORE-HOUSES

*

Apart from becoming more run down, the Marischal College fore-houses had
not changed in appearance since Byron's time. The archway, extreme left,
gave access to Ogstons' Court, the family home of the well-known Gallowgate
soap and candle manufacturer, Alexander 'Soapy' Ogston. His grandson,
Professor Sir Alexander Ogston, the pioneering surgeon in antiseptics, was
born there in 1844. The enlarged archway next to it, surmounted by the Earl
Marischal's coat-of-arms, led to the kirk and college close. Next door, the
ground floor of the house, gifted by Dr Guild, intended as a stationer's, had
become the College Gate Clothing (sometimes the fascia read 'Clothiery')
House. The entrepreneurial proprietor Henry Gray was in a substantial way
of business and as early as the 1870s had bought old premises on the corner
of Broad Street and the Gallowgate. These he later demolished and erected
'a commodious and handsome granite structure' as his gents' and boys' tailoring and outfitting department, naming it, with a whiff of a pun, 'Greyfriars
House'. (This building was purchased by Aberdeen University Court in 1933
and reconstructed as the University Union, J. B. Nicol, architect, opening in
1939. See page 87. It closed in 2004.)

*The Broad Street fore-houses ran in a terrace from Littlejohn Street at the north
end, left, to Queen Street at the south. From left, the Ogston's Court, and College
Court pends, the latter surmounted by the Earl Marischal's arms, Henry Gray's
clothiery and the reservoir with giant clock.*

The fore-houses, continued from overleaf. Picking up from the reservoir, with a fruiterer below, left, is the house with a central turret and Lord Byron's with the cart outside. The remaining houses running towards Queen Street have rarely been photographed.

Back in Broad Street, the upper level of the unusual building next door to Henry Gray, built in 1766, was the town's central reservoir. The lower part was the fire station, where the town's fire engines were stabled. The large clock that dominated the pediment was installed when Broad Street folk complained that the building 'shut up the clock on the college kirk from public view'. The introduction of Dee water in 1866 and the building of the Union Place water house (long since a bank) made the Broad Street reservoir redundant. The cisterns were sold off as scrap metal and the water house was adapted for stores and leased to Mr William Pyper. By the late nineteenth century S. Byres had a wholesale fruiterer's there.

Next was an interesting seventeenth-century house almost overwhelmed by its great central turret. The northern section of the house had a quaint bell-shaped tiled roof, not visible in all pictures. It had the usual Jamesone-style details, but was not a Jamesone. The architects MacGibbon & Ross found:

A certain individuality which marks it off from the others. It is a small building with a courtyard enclosed by an ashlar wall on the left side of the tower. The wall is very wavering and frail and in it there is a nicely moulded gateway.

*The turreted house in Broad Street, complete with interesting iron finial. On demolition the turret was carted off to embellish a country mansion (*Castellated and Domestic Architecture of Scotland, *MacGibbon & Ross Vol 5, 1892).*

The four-storey house next door, No. 64, built of dressed granite, probably by John Jeans, architect of the ultimate Bow Brig, was home to the Byron household, young George, his mother Catherine and their servant May Gray between 1791–8. They rented a six-room apartment on the first floor, comprising a spacious sitting room with three tall windows facing on to the street, a kitchen, three bedrooms and a dressing room. The landlord was a Mr Leslie, father of a well-known Aberdeen surgeon. 'Once again the Byron household was to live above a shop', wrote an American commentator on the move from Queen Street. In fact the great majority of Aberdeen's city dwellers lived over shops. The council chambers incorporated shops at ground level to provide revenue. More significant was the fact that the Byron apartment was rated at £13 annually, in the highest price bracket in town and in one of the most fashionable areas. Indeed it was rated more highly than the apartment of the famous Professor Beattie. The Byron rooms later became the printing offices of a Mr Rennie. The shop on the ground floor was tenanted for many years by Mr John Mackintosh LLD, author of *The History of Civilization in Scotland.*

The Second-largest
Granite Building in the World
*

The Broad Street fore-houses were demolished in 1902, part of the ambitious extension scheme of 1893–1905 when the magnificent west front of Marischal College was created, marking the Quatercentenary of Aberdeen University. Greyfriars Kirk, earmarked for demolition, came down in the spring of 1903 amidst bitter controversy. It was the only remaining pre-Reformation church in Aberdeen and the architect, A. Marshall Mackenzie, had prepared plans for its retention within the new scheme, to no avail.

A new Greyfriars Church was incorporated at the south end of the new frontage, and the framework of the great south window of the old kirk, its tracery and mullion, were built into its east end. In 1903 it was set with stained glass by C.E. Kempe The 'new' Greyfriars Church closed in 2006. During the second half of the twentieth century, the main focus of Aberdeen University activity moved to the 'mere village' of old Aberdeen. A notice outside Marischal College in 2007, the second largest granite frontage in the world, proclaims it as the 'new corporate headquarters' of Aberdeen City Council.

Greyfriars Kirk, right, sits miserably waiting demolition amidst the splendid new architecture of Marischal College with the burgeoning frontage, left and Mitchell Tower, rear, with Archibald Simpson's neatly capped towers on either side. The granite obelisk, in honour of Sir James McGrigor, Marischal graduate and father of the RAMC, was later moved to the Duthie Park.

Broad Street in September 1906 as Edward VII arrives to inaugurate the
Marischal College Extensions. A little arboretum of evergreens is an interesting feature,
and was attempted again in 2004. The new Greyfriars Kirk, centre left incorporated in
the pristine frontage, dominates the picture. It stands on the site of Patrick Christie's
Lodging (page 84). Just beyond the Kirk is the west end of Queen Street. The well known
pawn brokers, the Northern Loan Co, is at No 8, right of the Kirk which unfortunately
blocks out Byron's House at No 10. The gable-end, centre rear, was No 2 Queen Street,
Ewen & Co, cabinetmakers. It turned the corner to become No 34, the last building in
the Nos 12-34 Broad Street block demolished, like Queen Street, in 1973. (page 67). That
row is mostly hidden but back houses in the Queen Street courts can be glimpsed. To the
right opposite the townhouse clock tower, the dome of the Broad Street – Union Street
corner building is silhouetted. (page 187) It was demolished in 1970.

PATRICK CHRISTIE'S LODGING

*

The formation of Queen Street had encroached on the courtyard of Patrick Christie's Lodging, which presently found itself on the north side of the new street, at the corner with Broad Street. The building went over to commercial use in the nineteenth century and the *Aberdeen Herald* was edited there by the formidable James Adam. Even in its run-down state, the old house retained its wide ornamental doorway, fine stone staircase and rooms embellished with

Christie's Lodging predated Queen Street. It was a mid-seventeenth-century
L-shaped towerhouse with a corbelled-out single-storey stair turret with conical roof.
Patrick Christie had inscribed his initials on one of the skewputs and a projecting
spurstone bore the coats-of-arms of Christie and Milne, for his wife
(Old Landmarks of Aberdeen, *G Gordon Burr, 1885*).

carved timber and marble mantelpieces. It was pulled down in 1902 along with neighbouring Jopp's and Henderson's Courts to make way for the new Greyfriars Church at the south end of the Marischal College frontage.

BROAD STREET: WEST SIDE
*

Even as early as 1906, Robert Anderson, writing in *Aberdeen in Bygone Days*, noted of Broad Street that 'much of the west side has been remodelled or rebuilt'.

Nos 41–45 was the first head office of the North of Scotland Bank, from 1836, before the construction of their splendid edifice on the Castle Street/King Street corner. The tenants were bought out and extensive alterations and the purchase of furniture entrusted to the architect Archibald Simpson, not too lowly a chore apparently for the creator of the Granite City. 'Mr Gray of Edinburgh' had the most important task. He was instructed to construct the safe. The Old Bank House as it was later known was subsequently occupied by J & W Cameron, drapers, silk mercers, hatters and lace dealers. James and William were Kildrummy loons who made good. They later moved to more spacious premises at No. 75, near the Upperkirkgate end, while St Katherine's Club for Girls took over at No. 45. J & W Cameron later moved to Nos 179–85 George Street, developing their own specialities within the drapery trade. No. 75 Broad Street, extending back to the Guestrow was part of an impressive range of buildings acquired or built by the amazing Henry Gray of College

The tall building, Nos 41–5, about the middle of the row and later known as the Old Bank House, was not bonny but it had interesting occupants.

The west side of Broad Street in the 1920s. James Mutch, ironmongers, left, at No. 47, continued on from the Old Bank House. Blairton Lane, beyond the College Café, gave access to the Guestrow. No. 57, the old gable-end house fronting the street, was once the townhouse of James Milne of Blairton. At this time Alfred Ross, brush manufacturer, was on the ground floor. J & A Massie, cabinetmakers, at No. 65 was just beyond the lane. Massie took over rivals Robert Cumming next door at Nos 67–73. The splendid building to the extreme right, No. 75 was the emporium of Henry Gray, clothiers, later housing J & W Cameron, drapers.

Gate Clothing. Here he ran a department store specialising in a vast range of ladies' clothing, soft goods, furnishings and carpet manufacturing.

After the Second World War, the west side of Broad Street was demolished piecemeal over years to make way for what would be St Nicholas House, fortunately itself doomed to oblivion at time of writing. The Old Bank building went in 1945 and I recall years later, as a student, waiting for the bus to King's College at the Upperkirkgate end amidst what I vaguely assumed to be bomb damage, with cars parked on the empty ground. If I remember rightly, Mrs Agnes Norrie's furniture shop at No. 35, James Mutch, J & A Massie, and James G. Bisset, the university bookseller at No. 85, were among the last to go. Down at the south end, the block from the Netherkirkgate, turning into Union Street and then on to Union Wynd, which we met at the beginning of this chapter when it was occupied by hatters and a bookbinder, was latterly occupied by municipal offices. It was removed in 1970 for road-widening. That was the end of Broad Street on its west side.

THE GALLOWGATE

The Broadgate led on into the Gallowgate, first mentioned in 1350. Oddly, it never evolved into Gallows Street! It was about 800 yards long, narrow and hilly. It ended at the Gallowgate-head where the road branched, the left fork taking the northbound traveller to Inverurie while the right fork led to Old Aberdeen and so to Buchan. The Gallowgate Port, the city's finest, displaying the Royal Arms in colour, stood about two-thirds of the way down, straddling

The Gallowgate looking north in the early 1900s. Right, the buildings on the east side await demolition. The entrance to Littlejohn Street is just beyond the cart. Extreme left, Henry Gray's emporium, Greyfriar's House, with canopy and brattishing. The entrance was draped with clothes for sale, as was the custom. This building was reconstructed as the Students' Union in the 1930s.

the road on whose west side the Aberdeen College now sits. It would have commemorated the visits of James IV, passing down the Gallowgate to Old Aberdeen to observe the building of the college named in his honour. The port gave its name to Porthill, a once distinct area of the Gallowgate, though no more now than a gentle rise starting at the 'new' Berry Street. The gallows, possibly the earliest of the city's several hanging grounds, stood outside the port on the east side.

MAR'S CASTLE
*

Along with the Broadgate, the Gallowgate was Aberdeen's principal thoroughfare, where the north-east's finest had their lodgings, set in spacious feus with magnificent views, their 'tails' or long gardens sloping down to the Lochside on the west side and the Back Causeway on the east. Chief among them and a short distance within the Port was the L-shaped, red pantiled

Left. These views of Mar's Castle both date from the 1890s, shortly before demolition. The line drawing, from the north-west, from MacGibbon & Ross's Castellated and Domestic Architecture of Scotland, *Vol 5, 1892, concentrates on its noble features, the corbelled-out stair turret and the double corbel course.*

Right. The photograph from the south-west shows it as a multi-tenanted slum.

townhouse of the Earls of Mar. In date and style it resembled Provost Ross's House of 1593, with hallmarks of the work of Andrew Jamesone. The skewput on the front gable was dated 1595 and there was a coat-of-arms panel halfway up the front wall. It had two foreland tenements and a backland and its own close, Reid's Court, on the south side which led to the large garden and summer house. It was altered to its detriment in 1836 when repairs were carried out and the ground floor was given over to shops. In 1886 A.M. Munro, city chamberlain and historian wrote: 'Almost every foot of the garden is now occupied with houses scattered about in picturesque confusion.' By 1897 the town council had acquired Mar's Castle and pulled it down 'to improve the amenity'. Edward Meldrum called it 'an excellent example of a medieval townhouse'.

THE QUAKERS

*

Immediately to the south of Mar's Castle, though set behind it, was the Quakers' burial ground, acquired by the Society in 1660. They were subject to persecution in Aberdeen in the seventeenth century and the great stone dykes which enclosed the graveyard were again and again 'dinged doon' on the orders of the town council, who argued that the Quakers had not the right to

The Quaker meeting house in the Gallowgate, by J.A. Sutherland.

bury 'thair deed in their ain kailyaird'. In 1827, by then free of persecution for over a century, the Quakers built a plain and substantial meeting house in a court between Mar's Castle and their burial ground, at the highest point in the Gallowgate.

Some forty years later the Quakers moved to Diamond Street, and the old premises were used as a currying shop by John Watt & Son, leather merchants. It was swept away under the Gallowgate Improvement Scheme of 1907. The burial ground received a direct hit during the air raid of 1942 and so vanished all traces of the Quaker presence in the Porthill. Low-rise flats and Porthill and Seamount Courts now occupy the old Mar's Castle and Quaker lands.

The Porthill Factory
and its Neighbours
*

After the passing of the Town and Country Planning Act of 1947, there was an attempt to list the Gallowgate's remaining historic buildings, to little avail. Next to the site of Mar's Castle was the sternly handsome Porthill Factory, dating from around 1750. It formed a four-sided courtyard entered from Seamount Place through a gateway with a bell bracket above. The entrance door of the east range was reached by a double-curved staircase. It had been built as a factory for the Porthill Company but the venture soon failed and the

The Porthill Factory.

building was sold to Milne, Cruden & Co, linen manufacturers of ill repute. In a few years Milne, Cruden & Co moved to their new factory in Spring Garden and the Porthill Factory was occupied by Samuel Willans, stoneware merchant, and later by William Kitson, still remembered, who ran his china and glass warehouse there. It was demolished in 1960. The oldest remaining building in the Gallowgate stood next door to the Porthill Factory, the early eighteenth century No. 178 Gallowgate, built of granite boulders and gable-end to the street. Forestairs on the south side led to the upper house and an arched pend on the north side gave access to a courtyard and stables. There was a pub next door and another house with forestairs lay behind.

The Porthill Factory, No. 178, and its neighbours, including Aberdeen Lads' Club and the Gallowgate Church, which had survived bombing in 1942, were also razed to the ground in the early 1960s. Across the road, the whole of Innes Street, Young Street and Berry Street (formerly Lane) vanished to be replaced by a concrete fortress, the Aberdeen College. The Porthill-

No. 178 Gallowgate, by I.W. Davidson.

The Gallowgate looking down to Mounthooly around 1930.

Mounthooly end of the Gallowgate was swept away in the 1970s for a road improvement scheme that included the construction of the two-and-a-half-acre Mounthooly Roundabout.

GILBERT GERARD'S
MANSION

✳

Going back now to the Broad Street end of the Gallowgate, a piecemeal slum clearance programme of the early 1900s saw much of the east side cleared away, including the very fine mansion of Gilbert Gerard, advocate, erected in

ELEVATION.   SOUTH ELEVATION   *Room* A

Gilbert Gerard's mansion was two-storeyed, with a steep slated roof. Room A on the
first floor, the piano nobile, had fine wood panelling and a fireplace whose Ionic
pilasters and overmantle echoed the front door.

1787 by William Dauney, architect, who was Archibald Simpson's uncle. Gilbert Gerard's Mansion was built in the close that was called Poors' Hospital Court (No. 56 Gallowgate) after the house was sold as a girls' hospital in 1819. It was demolished in 1905 and cinders were laid on the site. Many a game of football was played there. In the mid-1950s the Ministry of Public Building and Works erected Greyfriars House, hailed as Aberdeen's ugliest office block, on the site of Gerard's mansion. In the 1990s, the façade was given a 'makeover' and it now masquerades as a classical temple.

THE MIDDLE SCHOOL
✳

A little north of the Gilbert Gerard site, Reid's Court near Littlejohn Street was demolished in 1877 to provide a site for the Middle School. It was Aberdeen School Board's fourth public school with a good educational reputation, with French, Latin, science and elocution on the curriculum as well as the basics. By the early twentieth century the building was extended, thanks to the removal of Ewen, Inglis and Union Courts. The Board's great pioneering achievement, and one for which it was criticised for extravagance, was the construction of the Middle Pond. Whoever heard of an east-end school having a swimming pool? Only the private Robert Gordon's College had such a resource at that time. Instruction, however, was available to council pupils

The Middle School in the 1970s, surrounded by signs of continuing demolition in the Gallowgate. The original school buildings are on the left. W. Ogg Allan, the architect of the 1907 extension above, sought something worthy of the magnificent new façade of its neighbour Marischal College, yet plain, strong, with a sense of grace and 'a feeling of appropriateness'.

throughout the city. Countless Aberdonians were taught to swim by the Middle's immortal instructor, Mr Pirie. The Middle became an Intermediate School in 1924, then a Junior Secondary. With a declining population in the area it closed in 1975, to the regret of many of its former pupils. It was demolished in the early 1990s.

OLD ST PAUL'S

*

The handsome pend gateway at No. 61 Gallowgate stood a little north of the junction of the Gallowgate and St Paul Street, almost opposite the Middle School. It gave access to the fashionable Episcopal Meeting House, old St Paul's Episcopal Chapel, dating from 1721, which lay in Chapel Court between the Gallowgate and Loch Street, and which gave its name to St Paul Street. Here too were the school and the manse. The architect of both the gateway and the chapel was Archibald Jaffray, a member of the well-known Kingswells Quaker family. The congregation came from the Gallowgate and Broadgate gentry and further afield. Here on 22 August 1773, Dr Samuel

St Paul's Gateway with its frame of rusticated Roman Doric pilasters, its upper part embellished with a fanlight of wrought iron. This perished in the post-war period, after making unfortunate contact with a lorry.

St Paul's Chapel from the Gallowgate gateway, with the school, right. The north wing to the right of the chapel was designed in 1764 by the neighbourhood architect, William Littlejohn.

Johnson and James Boswell attended holy communion during their stay in Aberdeen. The future Lord Byron attended reluctantly, dragged by his mama. Francis Peacock the dancing master was a member, and James Ross was organist. The chapel was demolished and the new St Paul's Episcopal Church built in 1865, with entrance from Loch Street, next door to the Northern Co-operative Arcade. It too was attended by high society and had its own carriage drive. It had closed by 1970 and stood deserted for some sixteen years prior to demolition. St Paul's Gateway was 'saved' and relocated to Loch Street, where it sits anonymously in a small enclosure.

THE FINAL DEMOLITIONS

*

The demolition of buildings on the west side of the Gallowgate immediately north of St Paul Street, mostly B-listed as being of considerable historical interest, was authorised by the Secretary of State in 1981 to make way for the Bon Accord Centre and took place in 1986. Among them were No. 47 and Nos 49–51, late eighteenth and early nineteenth century respectively. Nos 53–57 and Nos 59–3 were both eighteenth century, the former group including the St Paul's Gateway to Chapel Court where the C-listed manse was demolished. At Nos 65–75 the Northern Co-operative's Gallowgate frontage was also pulled down. These buildings had been the site of Dingwall's Court and the handsome eighteenth-century town lodging of John Dingwall, provost of Aberdeen from 1799–1800. Others further north had been demolished earlier.

The former front office of 'Soapy Ogston's' (Ogston & Tennant Soap and Candle Manufacturers) at No. 111 Gallowgate, and by the 1960s the City Taxis office, survived, though not the industrial buildings to the rear.

Opposite top.
The buildings from No 47 to No 75 Gallowgate await demolition in 1986.
St Paul's Gateway is prominent on the left.

Opposite below.
The same scene viewed from Loch Street, including the inner
side of St Paul's Gateway (a good example of an arched pend) during demolition.
Marischal College's Mitchell Tower rises to the right.

An interesting piece of industrial archaeology. The former Ogston & Tennant factory, later the City Taxis' forecourt, see p.96, viewed from Loch Street, was also demolished.

CHAPTER 4

THE KIRKGATES
AND THE GUESTROW

THE NETHERKIRKGATE

The Gallowgate has taken us up to the edge of the town. We can turn back now and explore the area west of Broad Street, the Kirkgates, leading to the Mither Kirk of St Nicholas. The Netherkirkgate, the nether or lower road to

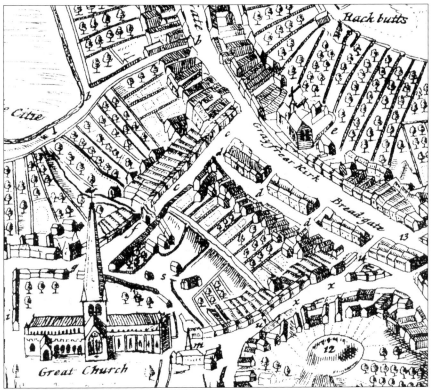

The Netherkirkgate is (x) in Gordon's Plan, the Upperkirkgate (c).
The Guestrow (d) lies between. The Mitherkirk is bottom left.

99

St Nicholas Kirk, first appears in the records in 1382. The eastern starting point was at the south end of the Guestrow, roughly, in modern terms, from the old Bond Bar, now the Ilicit Still. It was a short street running westwards, straddled near the top of Flourmill Lane by the Netherkirkgate Port, (u) on Gordon's Plan. Some twenty yards west of the Port, roughly opposite the present Old Frigate Bar, the road split. The left fork became Putachieside, later Carnegie's Brae, and sloped down to the Green and the start of the Shiprow. The Netherkirkgate continued as the right-hand fork, passing the Town's Hospital (m) on the Plan, with the little spire, alias St Thomas's Hospital, alias the Guild Brethren's Hospital, a retirement home catering in the seventeenth century for 'fyve or six honest decayit brethren of guild'. It was taken down in the mid-eighteenth century. The curious twin-gabled building in front of it was the Wallace Tower, though it is not a very recognisable representation. Beyond was the old choir of the Mither Kirk, the East Kirk of St Nicholas, as it became after the Reformation, with Dubbie Raw, whose name indicated its nature, running in front.

BENHOLM'S LODGING ALIAS
THE WALLACE TOWER
*

The land where the road forked was old Templar property, acquired in 1588 by Sir Robert Keith of Benholm, a younger brother of the Earl Marischal, founder of Marischal College. Benholm seems to have adhered to the same 'thay haf said' school of philosophy as his brother. The latter, in his ambassadorial capacity, had been instrumental in bringing about the marriage of James VI and Princess Anne of Denmark. As a token of gratitude James granted the Earl the Abbey of Deer and its revenues, provoking Benholm's envy and culminating in his seizing the Abbey in 1590.

A truce was eventually arranged, but more outrageous behaviour on Benholm's part followed in 1593 when he took possession of a house of his brother's in Caithness. That was the year that the Earl founded Marischal College, and it may be that Benholm was again consumed with jealousy. Though he already owned property in Aberdeen and did not lack somewhere to stay, he built a town lodging on his new land at the Netherkirkgate-Putachieside fork. The site chosen was an awkward one, and Benholm's Lodging was no douce townhouse. It was a Z-plan fortified towerhouse, complete with gun loops, with dimensions similar to contemporary Donside castles such as Terpersie, Asloun and Pitcaple. The body of the castle was

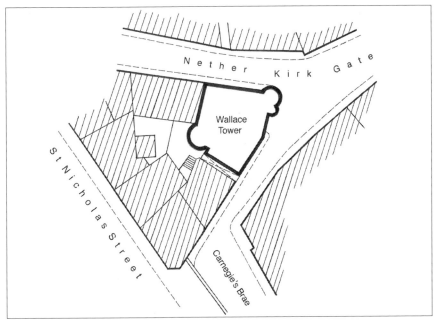

The Wallace Tower. Its appearance was deceptive, its dimensions more considerable than might have been expected.

almost square in shape and the two round towers sitting in the south-west and north-east corners completed the Z shape. Between them, the towers and the gun port commanded the Netherkirkgate Port, the Green, the Bow Brig, the Denburn estuary, the harbour, the Broadgate and the Gallowgate. The north-east tower, capped by a conical, tiled roof and set well forward from the Putachieside and Netherkirkgate ranges, dominated the road junction.

The interior comprised a hall with a basement below, chambers on the first floor and attics above. The second, south-west tower, invisible from the street, was a flat-roofed stair tower overlooking the garden and the courtyard whose outer wall sloped down Carnegie's Brae. Benholm's Lodging was one of the best-known landmarks in the town, thanks to the figure of the vigilant armed man that stood in large recess at first-floor level of the north-east tower, his sword over his left shoulder, ready to challenge anyone walking along the Netherkirkgate from the Guestrow. It resembled sculpted figures of the same period at other castles, at Fyvie, Tolquhoun and Edzell, while the early seventeenth-century dress and armour point to a likeness of Sir Robert Keith himself. A carved stag's head, the heraldic beast of the Keiths, was set just above the recess and further round the tower, in full view of those walking along the Netherkirkgate from the East Kirk, was an armorial panel

The Wallace Tower with the brae of Putachieside, left, and the Netherkirkgate, right, leading on to St Nicholas Kirk.

with the shield of Keiths. A triangular dormer window-head or tympanum bore the initials SRKB, Sir Robert Keith of Benholm, which ensured that everyone knew to whom the towerhouse belonged and at the same time silently challenged his brother and his college.

Fortunately no blood was shed between the Keith brothers and they were later reconciled. After Robert's death in 1616 the Earl Marischal acquired the lands of Benholm, possibly including the towerhouse, which was made available to Patrick Dun, owner of Ferryhill and benefactor of the Grammar School. Dun, one-time mediciner at King's College and later principal of Marischal College, lived in the Tower during the Earl Marischal's lifetime. Later residents included several distinguished local families and eventually in 1768 a snuff and tobacco merchant, John Niven. By this time the lodging was called the Wallace Neuk (or Nook) as well as Benholm's Lodging. The memory of Sir Robert was growing dim and the warlike statue inspired the new name, though there was never any connection with the Guardian of Scotland. Niven added a south wing, extending the frontage down Carnegie's Brae and building over the original courtyard. Here he kept his kiln and other equipment for snuff and tobacco manufacture, and on the first floor built a well-proportioned business room, panelled in Scots pine. At some point, the statue's sword came loose and was replaced in a more pacific manner, pointing downwards.

In the late eighteenth century, Parliament, as an anti-smuggling measure, prohibited the manufacture of snuff within three miles of the sea. This may have caused the Nivens to sell up and settle in Peebles, for by 1789 James Coutts, flax dresser, was owner. The following year we find him advertising in the *Aberdeen Journal*: 'To let the house of Wallace Nook. Seven Rooms. Apply Jas. Coutts at Wallace Nook'. After Coutts, John Donald Taylor and his heirs owned the property from 1851. Pictorial evidence shows that although the building had gone over to multiple tenancy, it was well kept and the walls regularly harled. In 1895, James Pirie, a spirit dealer, bought the premises and the building became the Wallace Tower pub, and so it remained for the rest of its existence. There were drastic alterations. The hall, kitchen and wide, arched fireplace were all removed. The bar's cellar was fitted up in the basement with the bar and public house on the floor above. Entry was from No. 63 Netherkirkgate. The rest of the building, which in 1918 was acquired by the city council, was partitioned into tenement flats.

Before the Second World War the pub was the favoured houff of a group of medical students, the OH Club, who were active in Charities Week and the Students' Show. The OH symbol indicates the alcoholic group in chemistry, and club members wore a small silver tankard as a lapel badge. They met at the table in the window alcove below the statue and remember the bar as a smallish, dark room. The group faded away, surviving members recall, as 'the Wallace Tower became less attractive and studies took up more time'. The Wallace Tower had become rundown, though following the Town and Country (Scotland) Act of 1947 it was listed in Category B as a building of historic and architectural merit. It was felt to be in safe hands. The last days of the Wallace Tower are best discussed in context with St Nicholas Street.

THE GUESTROW

The Guestrow ran between the Netherkirkgate and the Upperkirkgate and its shape (d and downwards in the plan at the beginning of this chapter) did not change much from Parson Gordon's time until the end. It was one of the oldest streets in Aberdeen, noted in 1450, the *vicus dict le Gastrow* or the *vicus lemurum* – the way of the spirits. The ghosts in question were those that haunted the neighbouring kirkyard of St Nicholas. By the eighteenth century the Guestrow was partly bounded to the west by Flourmill Lane, which went about two-thirds of the way along it from the Netherkirkgate, before finding the mill burn in its way. A left turn and a scramble down Flourmill Brae took one to the Dubbie Raw and St Nicholas Kirk.

THE EAST SIDE

THE RUSSEL HEAD
*

The houses on the east side backed on to those on the west side of the
Broadgate. Ragg's Lane, almost directly opposite Queen Street, and Blairton
Lane, opposite the Marischal College entrance were the two accesses to the
Guestrow from Broad Street. Parson Gordon has conveniently put his (d)
opposite each, though these lanes were not so named in his time. Ragg's Lane
took its name from Bailie Alexander Ragg, who owned land there in the early
eighteenth century. In the later nineteenth century, No. 35 Broad Street on
the Ragg's Lane corner was the home of a sculptor, George Russel, a skilled
if eccentric carver of ships' figureheads. His family were confectioners and a
bakery operated from the basement of his corner property. The authorities
closed it down because of insanitary conditions and Russel was convinced,
probably wrongly, that a neighbour, an ironmonger named Alexander
Stephen, had informed on him. He sculpted a self-portrait in the style of a
ship's figurehead, an angry, twisted, bearded face shouting silent abuse, and
stuck it in a prominent corner to annoy Stephen every time he passed.

THE BLAIRTON STONE
*

Blairton Lane took its name from James Milne, Dean of Guild, who owned
the estate of Blairton in the late seventeenth and early eighteenth centuries.
No angry heads there, but Blairton's gable-ended townhouse, facing Broad
Street, and a very fine heraldic stone with the date 1701.

THE WEST SIDE

The more substantial houses on the west side sat gable-end to the Guestrow
and there were numerous pends which took one through to houses standing
in their own cobbled courts, with long gardens sloping towards the Mither
Kirk. This was a fashionable place to live from the sixteenth century until
well into the nineteenth century. It was the home of lairds, generals, provosts,
bishops, burgesses, bailies, advocates, architects, doctors, dowagers, magistrates, merchants, Jacobites, Hanoverians, Quakers and Episcopalians. We
can start at the Netherkirkgate end and work towards the Upperkirkgate.

Ragg's Lane from the Guestrow by I. W. Davidson.

105

ARCHIBALD SIMPSON'S HOUSE
✳

Archibald Simpson, the architect, was born at No. 15 Guestrow in 1790. It was designed around 1786 by his uncle, William Dauney. The exterior was plain but there was good interior plasterwork and pine panelling. His father William Simpson, a Kincardineshire man, had a tailor's business, Simpson & Whyte, in partnership with his brother and Baillie John Whyte. Their premises were at No. 21 Union Street (Union Buildings), where the Shiprow enters Union Street. Baillie Galen, who owned much of the property in this part of the Guestrow, also owned the Union Buildings' feu and lived in spacious rooms above the Simpson's tailor's shop. Archibald had been well placed to win the contract for the Union Buildings.

No. 17 Guestrow next door, Baillie Galen's former home, became, from 1838, the first office of Aberdeen Savings Bank, 'open every Thursday, Friday and Saturday from Nine to Ten o'clock Morning and Seven to Eight o'clock Evening both for the receipt and repayment of Deposits'. The bank moved to a new building in Exchange Street twenty years later.

Above. Archibald Simpson's birthplace at No. 15 Guestrow. After studying in London, France and Germany, he returned to Aberdeen and set up practice there in 1813.

Left. Blairton Lane from Broad Street looking west into the Guestrow. It makes an interesting comparison with the later illustration on page 86. At No. 57, Milne of Blairton's old townhouse, Alfred Ross, brush manufacturer, has not yet got his fascia up.

Aberdeen Savings Bank's first office, at No. 17 Guestrow, left. The Shepherd's Court
Gateway can be seen beyond. Across the road a house, curving at the corner, marks the
junction of the Guestrow and Ragg's Lane. The block beyond, from Blairton Lane to the
Upperkirkgate, is set forward of the others. By W.H. Murray.

THE GUESTROW COURTS

✳

The Shepherd's Court Gateway at No. 21 Guestrow was a magnificent
moulded sandstone arch leading to two houses owned in the seventeenth
century by Andrew Thomson, sheriff depute and advocate. A tablet inscribed
'AT 1673 AD' is probably a marriage stone, for a first son was born to Thomson
and his wife Agnes Divie in 1674. Inside Shepherd's Court, the turret-capped
stair tower, shown overleaf, is the entrance to the main house. After

Right.
The Shepherd's Court Gateway. The court was called Galen's Court
when the ubiquitous baillie owned it.

SHEPHERD'S COURT, GUESTROW, ABERDEEN. 12,586. G.W.W.

Thomson's death in 1690 Sir Andrew Bannerman of Elsick acquired the property. His son Patrick Bannerman was the city's short-lived Jacobite provost, from 1715–16, 'a gentlemanly man' who was not too concerned when the city ministers continued to pray for George I. He presented an address to the Old Pretender at Fetteresso and was knighted by him, but alas, was taken prisoner and incarcerated at Carlisle after the suppression of the Rising. He was sentenced to death but in the end was discharged.

The second house at Shepherd's Court was a side house and was used by the Episcopalians, under the leadership of their future bishop, John Skinner, as a meeting place in the days following the Forty-Five Rebellion.

Thornton Place, No. 29 Guestrow, accessed through a pend, was a large tenement house with shaped stairs and a handrail leading up to the entrance. Beyond was Thornton Court, No. 37, in the very heart of the Guestrow, leading down to Flourmill Lane. The Niven family, who had the small estate of Thornton, near Keith-Hall, Inverurie, owned these properties. John Niven, merchant, head of the family at the time of the Forty-Five, took part in the

Above left. Milner's Close was at No. 25. In its latter day photographs,
it appeared as dingy as the rest of the Guestrow but those who remember
it found it 'a pleasant little court'.

Above right. Thornton Place.

Left. No. 1 Shepherd's Court with its pepperpot stair tower.
The gateway is seen at the rear.

Inverurie Skirmish. He was imprisoned in the tolbooth and then taken to
Carlisle, tried and executed. His young son John was imprisoned with him,
but survived. He later made a fortune in the tobacco trade and remained an
ardent Jacobite all his life. We have met him already; it was he who bought
the Wallace Tower in 1768. It may have been at Thornton Court that Major

*Above. This is Mitchell's Court, No. 43 Guestrow, which lay between Thornton Place
and Duthie's Court. The tall tenement of inland and the house with the steps were built
by George Turner of Menie sometime in the early seventeenth century.*

Left. Thornton Court.

General Macdonald gave a party in 1807, in honour of the Duchess of Manchester and the Marquis of Huntly, whose arms 'were elegantly emblazoned on a transparency over the supper room door'.

THE VICTORIA MODEL LODGING HOUSE
✳

I had better confess. This building has been inserted under false pretences. It is an almost lost, and like Provost Ross's House, shows what can be done to restore a building that seemed beyond recall. Scarcely recognisable in this illustration, Sir George Skene's Mansion, dating from 1545, the finest townhouse in Aberdeen, is the only survivor of the Guestrow Clearances. Though

A junk-filled Duthie's Court and the Victoria Model Lodging House at No. 45 Guestrow. From the 1770s until 1885 it was in the ownership of the Duthie family, of later Duthie Park fame.

it had a fascinating past, a handsome exterior and rich internal décor, it became very run down in its latter-day role as doss-house and was, in any case, earmarked for demolition in 1932 along with the rest of the Guestrow.

QUAKERS' COURT
*

The Quakers left the Gallowgate for the Guestrow and built a modest meeting house, No. 53 Guestrow, the close naturally becoming Quakers' Court. It adjoined Skene's Mansion, of which A.M. Munro provides this curious piece of information:

> Apparently [Skene's] house was at one time in possession of the Jaffrays, a noted Quaker family and in proof of this there was still to be seen outside the house, the sarcophagus consisting of four massive blocks of granite clamped together, in which members of the Society of Friends were buried during the rigorous persecution which at one time denied them Christian burial.

During the Duke of Cumberland's unwelcome stay at Skene's Mansion en route to Culloden, a mint was set up in Quakers' Court, presumably to pay, not his much put-upon hosts, but the Hanoverian Army.

BARNETT'S CLOSE
AND THE DISPENSARY
*

Barnett's Close lay beyond Quakers' Court. It ran the breadth of the Guestrow, providing a short cut from St Nicholas Street to Broad Street via Flourmill Brae and Blairton Lane. It featured in an interesting 'for sale' advertisement of 1794:

> Houses and offices on the west side of the Guestrow lately possessed by the deceased Mrs Black of Cloghill, with the large garden adjoining which extends to Barnett's Close on the south, and to the miln burn on the west.

This handsome house, in plain coursed granite in a delightful, tree-lined setting, never fully built over, was acquired by John Abercrombie who had

The Dispensary, formerly the townhouse of the Blacks of Cloghill.

been provost from 1787–9. Nearly a century later, in 1871, the wandering caravan of the General Dispensary, Vaccine and Lying-in Institution moved out of Charles Court, Upperkirkgate, and came to rest at the former townhouse of the Blacks of Cloghill, where it continued its good work for nearly a hundred years. The house was much extended and a separate maternity hospital was built in the grounds. The Dispensary itself opened out into Stewart's Place and beyond lay the back-houses of the Upperkirkgate. We have reached journey's end.

THE LAST DAYS
*

By the 1830s a diverse society frequented the Guestrow. The anatomist Dr Andrew Moir, hailed as the founder of the School of Anatomy at Aberdeen University, is thought to have lived in a part of Skene's Mansion and on one occasion in 1831 the mob attempted to break down his door, using a huge paving slab as a battering ram. Fortunately they were prevailed on to desist. This would have been a good story for William Forsyth of the *Aberdeen Journal* and James Adam of the *Herald*, who spent the evening before their respective weeklies hit the streets closeted in a Guestrow howff, slaving over their leading articles. At No. 35 Robert Cobban published various journals

Demolition in the Guestrow, by W.S. Percy.

including the *Aberdeen Star*. By the 1850s the residents included tradesmen, tailors, a music teacher and numerous spirit dealers. Alexander Reith Gray from Oldmeldrum came to Aberdeen to seek his fortune and in 1857 set up his own company as a wine and spirit merchant in the Guestrow. He prospered and A.R. Gray Ltd became a household name in Aberdeen.

By the end of the nineteenth century, the medieval thoroughfare of the Guestrow and its courts and gardens had degenerated into a tough, over-crowded, airless ghetto nicknamed the Gush, where policemen went in pairs. Flourmill Lane was crammed with narrow tenements, cheek by jowl. The greater part of the area was demolished in the Guestrow Scheme of 1930–32, intended not only to clear away the slums but also to widen Broad Street and to prepare the site for new municipal buildings.

There was a hiatus in 1932. A debate had broken out over the fate of No. 45, Skene's once glorious mansion, that house of many names. Miss Elizabeth Duthie had leased it to the managers of the Victoria Model Lodging House, but when they moved to West North Street, No. 45, under different manage-ment, declined into a common (rather than a model) lodging house, nick-named in memory of the Duke of Cumberland, the least model of its lodgers. This is not the place to recall its early, rich history, for it has survived (though only by a whisker) thanks to the intervention and persistence of the Lord Lyon, Sir Thomas Innes of Learney, Dr W. Douglas Simpson, Moultrie R.

Kelsall and many others, and especially of Queen Elizabeth, the late Queen Mother, who may well have been alerted to the situation by one of these illustrious gentlemen. After the war it was magnificently restored by the city council, Edward Meldrum, architect, and was opened to the public by Her Majesty in 1953. It was 'the fulfilment of a dream I have cherished,' she said. Sheriff Thomson's arch had been saved in the nick of time, taken down and reassembled in Union Terrace Gardens in 1931. The Russel Head and Milne of Blairton's heraldic stone had all been preserved, as was a finely carved oak frieze from No. 43a at Mitchell's Court. They all returned, though not of course to their original positions. Sheriff Thomson's travelling arch can be seen outside Skene's Mansion, as can the Russel Head, scolding from the south-east wall.

The Dispensary at Barnett's Close, fulfilling a vital service, was reprieved for a time. I remember attending the Schools' Eye Clinic when it functioned there and being surprised to find this attractive old house in a tree-lined garden in the middle of a wasteland in the city centre. It was

Above. Flourmill Lane in the course of demolition, viewed from Flourmill Brae. The side entrance of the Equitable is right; Skene's Mansion towers in the distance.

Left. To the delight of local children, Codona's Carnival moved into the cleared section of the Guestrow. This was quite an event. Florence Meredith recalls watching the carnival lights from the window of the family's third-floor flat in Cruden's Court, Broad Street: 'It was very exciting with brightly lit roundabouts and smoke from the generators.'

demolished in the mid-'6os and at the same time Skene's Mansion closed for a long period while the local government offices, St Nicholas House, was being built. It opened again in 1972. From the cosy security of Duthie's Court in the nineteenth century, to a new setting in a landscaped pleasance in the 1960s, the mansion now found itself in the middle of a concrete jungle. Those approaching it from the south-west found that Flourmill Lane had become a concrete passageway, awkwardly splayed at the Netherkirkgate end.

THE UPPERKIRKGATE

The detail from Gordon's Plan at the beginning of this chapter shows the Upperkirkgate (c) – or Overkirkgate as the parson called it – the upper or high road to the great St Nicholas Kirk, running westwards from Broadgate to meet Schoolhill. On the northern side there are already a handful of backhouses and gardens stretching back to what remains of the loch. 'The Lane called the Vennell' is (b), which continues on to the Lochside, later Loch Street. The Upperkirkgate Port is (f). It was an early police station, the burgh's guard being based in a room above the gates. It was also one of the many places where Samuel Rutherford, the famous preacher, lived when banished to Aberdeen in 1636– 8. The Port, the last to go, was demolished in 1794.

THE SOUTH SIDE:
COMPLETELY LOST
*

In Parson Gordon's time, the south side of the Upperkirkgate, much taken up by Guestrow gardens, was scarcely developed. By the eighteenth century it was well developed and by the nineteenth, filled with sturdy tenements with shops on the ground floor.

Right. The south side of the Upperkirkgate, seen below Marischal College, c. 1910. The building at No. 41 stuck out into the pavement and pedestrians had to step onto the street to avoid it. The house with the hipped roof at the end of St Nicholas Street, centre, was later and for a long time a branch of Boots the Chemist. Schoolhill is in the fore-ground. St Nicholas Kirkyard is extreme right. Matthews & Mackenzie's handsome row of tenements is on the left, Wordie's pend, leading to Donald's Court, extreme left. James Rust's turret of 1891 challenges the north tower of the Marischal College frontage and the Mitchell Tower beyond. Below the turret, on the ground floor was a wee, men-only bar.

Left, the south side of the Upperkirkgate in its heyday, from the etching by
EB MacKinnon, 1918. Right, 1951 and the last buildings are about to be carted off in
the back of a lorry. Beyond, the Schoolhill range of Reid & Pearson's can be glimpsed.

The south side was never as grand as the north side and was demolished for road-widening and redevelopment during the early 1950s, the upper half going first. Minus its south side, the Upperkirkgate lost its cosy ambience though the empty area was initially planted out as an arboretum. By the 1970s the trees and the view had gone, the open space filled by a toilet block, by the north end of the St Nicholas Centre and other bits of concrete.

THE NORTH SIDE:
ALMOST LOST

*

Between the seventeenth and the early nineteenth centuries the fashionable north side of the Upperkirkgate was graced by the townhouses of county lairds and city burgesses: the Davidsons of Cairnbrogie, the Andersons of Bourtie, the Robertsons of Glasgoego, Bailie Alexander, the Irvines of Hilton, the Cruickshanks of Banchory and General Hay, who hosted elegant parties. In 1792 the house of Mr John Annand there was advertised for sale, 'largely lately rebuilt, with public rooms large and elegant, suitable for a large family'. Some of the houses were superior tenements, and craftsmen and 'mechanics' were working in the area. In September 1778, James Law

Jeweller, Upperkirkgate, 'trained by the best dentists in London' was advertising that he made artificial teeth. Some had their workshops in the extensive hinterland of courts behind the Upperkirkgate houses.

As time passed the Upperkirkgate lost its upper-class cachet, but the frontages, mostly shops on the ground-floor level and flats above, remained a varied and valued part of the townscape.

Part of the section of the Upperkirkgate which escaped demolition. The 'reprieved' section included the gable-ended 'Wedding Bell' building, centre. McCall's the antique dealers at Nos 48–50, second left from the 'Bell', had four arcade-style arches openings; the shop door, with its eye-catching old-style display of kilts and Highland weaponry, two shop windows and the pend leading to Burn Court. The premises were owned by the Hawthorne family who lived above the shop in a handsomely restored three-storey flat. The backland buildings behind the frontages and beyond the turret building, extreme left, as far as the Northern Co-op/John Lewis ziggurat, right rear, have already been demolished, and the line of George Street obliterated. The 'bomb site' behind the turret building, extreme left, was Donald's Court.

The CCDA

*

By the early 1960s the city council (during the period that followed it changed its name from Aberdeen Corporation to Aberdeen City District Council) decided to redevelop, in partnership with property developers, an area of 11.44 acres centred on St Nicholas Street and George Street. A 'clean sweep' of the area, demolishing it in one fell swoop – derelict buildings and those in good condition – was upheld as the only feasible policy and a Central Comprehensive Development Area (CCDA) was duly created, armed with extensive powers of acquisition.

To create the 'clean sweep' the south sides of the Upperkirkgate and Schoolhill were earmarked for destruction even though six of the Upperkirkgate's thirteen buildings were listed. Nos 24–6, dating from 1694, with its corbelled skews and sundials, was said to have been a provost's residence while its contemporary, No. 42, for long the 'Wedding Bell', was one of the few surviving buildings in Aberdeen with a gable-end to the street. The local authority view was:

> The buildings ... are in reasonably good condition but cannot be absorbed into the redevelopment without severe detriment to the latter and their retention would not appear to be justified.

There was anger and concern from the residents, from heritage societies, and from many other quarters, over the loss of a so valued a piece of townscape. Eventually, at the end of 1974 the Upperkirkgate and Schoolhill frontages were reprieved.

The Courts
of the Upperkirkgate

*

The backland courts of the Upperkirkgate were doomed to extinction. The official view was:

> Much of the land behind the shopping frontages is unused or derelict. The area cannot function efficiently as a commercial area due to the presence of buildings which are outworn and not suitable for modern purposes and land uses not in keeping with the function of the area.

Upperkirkgate residents and many others were convinced of a policy to blight the area, pointing out property that had been acquired by the local authority and then neglected. As the journalist Cuthbert Graham, normally the mildest of men, wrote in 1974: 'The "derelict areas" behind are largely due to the planning blight which the corporation itself created and which has persisted for some seven years.'

The Upperkirkgate courts had their share of shabby tenements, but were also hives of local light industry. The six easterly closes Wilson's, Clark's Ross's, Ironmonger's, later Kirkgate, Farquhar's and Bourtie's which became Boy's Hospital, ran north towards St Paul Street, as the Vennel became in 1842, though not usually arriving there. Next came Drum's Lane, originally entered by a pend and running from the Upperkirkgate through to the junction of Loch Street and St Paul Street. The remaining three closes, Charles, Crown and Burn, all ran towards Loch Street.

PROVOST ROBERTSON'S HOUSE, ROSS'S COURT

*

Going back to the Broad Street end, Wilson's Court's was obliterated when Henry Gray bought the corner properties to create his clothiers emporium (the future Students' Union site). Moving downhill, George Leslie, provost in 1685–7 erected a house, Nos 6–8 Upperkirkgate, whose pend, Ross's Court, gave access to the garden. Leslie's house later passed to Alexander Robertson of Glasgoego, provost three times from 1740–57, who added a wing along the west side of Ross's Court, encroaching on the garden. Its chief feature was that great Aberdeen favourite, the pepperbox turret with roped corbelling. Inside it a stone stair led to a secret chamber near the top, a hidey-hole where the provost could conceal himself from irate burghers. The doorway to the tower bore the provost's name, that of his wife Jean Strachan, the date 1730 and above that the Robertson coat-of-arms with the punning Latin motto, *Robore et Sapore*, by strength and prudence.

By the 1860s the garden at Ross's Court had vanished under a mini-industrial complex, tenanted by George Goldie, 'airated water manufacturer', a tinsmith and a furniture dealer. By 1899 Provost Leslie's original forehouse and the back wing of Provost Roberston's back-house were demolished to make way for the headquarters and printing works of the newly formed Aberdeen University Press (AUP). Some of the original Robertson masonry was preserved for embellishment and the handsome new frontage echoed the

Ross's Court looking towards the Upperkirkgate. The 1730 wing of
Provost Robertson's House, right. The coat of arms can be glimpsed above
the side door and the stair tower is above.

Scots College in Paris. Ross's Court and Clark's Court echoed to the noise of printing presses as the works took up their length right through to St Paul Street. AUP relocated to Farmers' Hall Lane in 1963, was acquired by Robert Maxwell and after a couple of reincarnations, vanished.

IRONMONGER'S, LATER KIRKGATE COURT

*

The next court was Ironmonger's at No. 14 Upperkirkgate, where David Rowell, 'wholesale ironmonger, manufacturer and manufacturer of nails' took up residence soon after 1850. He had been a partner in Aberdeen Comb Works in its early, Stewart & Rowell, days, but parted company from John Stewart. He was succeeded at No. 14 by other ironmongers. The court, immediately east of the present Kirkgate Bar, was later appropriately renamed.

BOURTIE'S, LATER
BOYS' HOSPITAL COURT

*

This close, originally Bourtie's, was one of the oldest in the Upperkirkgate. Patrick Anderson of Bourtie and his wife Elizabeth Ogilvie built a plain three-storey townhouse at the far end of the close in 1741, their pride in ownership demonstrated by a modest inscription on the skewputts with their initials and the date. Anderson's forebear, Skipper John Anderson of Torry, had a title to land in the area by 1659 and the family acquired much surrounding property over the years. In 1828 Alexander Anderson rouped it all to David Gill and John Farquhar, who had given his name to nearby Farquhar's Court. The pair had set up as paint manufacturers and brassfounders. Farquhar & Gill sold off the Anderson townhouse, surplus to their needs at the time, to the managers of the Gallowgate-based orphanage, the Boys' Hospital, who were looking for 'more convenient premises' and the name of the court changed to Boys' Hospital. The Hospital later amalgamated with the Girls' Hospital and in 1871 moved to a splendid custom-built building in King Street, (later the 'Dough' School, the RGIT Offshore Survival Unit and now Meridian Court). The Anderson townhouse, which had acquired a curious semi-circular bow wing facing towards St Paul Street, was bought back by Farquhar & Gill and incorporated in their paint manufactory, which had now expanded so far north that it was overlooked by children in the classrooms of St Paul Street School, which fronted on to Loch Street.

*A mansion of many names: Anderson of Bourtie's Townhouse, the Boys' Hospital,
and here, part of the Farquhar & Gill North of Scotland Colour Works.
It was demolished in 1977.*

DRUM'S LANE
*

Just west of Boys' Hospital Court was Drum's Lane. In 1633 Marion Douglas,
widow of Alexander Irvine of Drum, mortified 3,000 merks to the town
council 'to bigg or buy ane commodious house in Aberdeen' to support
widows of burgesses and 'aged virgins' born within the burgh, provided they
were free of any public scandal. There was enough in the kitty to begin the
building of a house and the laying out of a garden in 1671. It was later discontinued and in 1800 Drum's Lane was laid out partly on the garden ground of
the Lady of Drum's Hospital, linking Upperkirkgate with Loch Street at its
junction with the Vennel or St Paul Street.

Farquhar & Gill was a very large concern. In their North of Scotland
Colour Works they manufactured a vast range of paint and enamel stains,

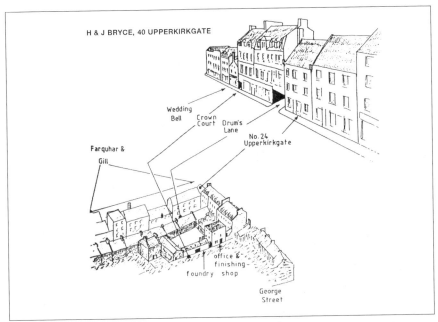

Sketch of H & J Bryce's premises at
40 Upperkirkgate/2 Crown Court, by I.B.D. Bryce.

varnishes, oils, compositions for painting ships' bottoms and much more. Their shop was at the former provost's house, No. 24 Upperkirkgate, and at No. 2 Drum's Lane, where they had extensive premises which carried on parallel to Boys' Hospital Court, and as far east as Ironmongers'/Kirkgate Court. On the south side of Drum's Lane were two late-eighteenth-century houses, Nos 5 and 7. According to Edward Meldrum, one had Adam-type doorways, semi-circular fanlights and rainwater heads finely executed in ornamental leadwork. It may have been the residence of the famous Professor James Beattie, whom we last met in the Lemon Tree.

Though the Farquhar & Gill partnership was dissolved in 1878, David Gill continued the paint and varnish side under the old name. Colonel W.S. Gill, who succeeded to the firm, was not your average painter and decorator but a keen territorial soldier whose family had a reputation for marrying well. His daughter, Ruth, married Edmund Roche, Lord Fermoy, and their daughter Frances married Earl Spencer. We all know whom their daughter, Lady Diana Spencer, married.

James Farquhar continued the brass-founding side of the business and on his death, his foreman brass-finisher, Hugh Bryce, set up with his cousin as H & J Bryce, Plumbers, Coppersmiths, Brass-Founders and Finishers.

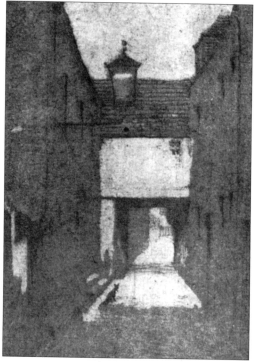

Charles Court.

They worked from No. 40 Upperkirkgate/2 Crown Court below Drum's Lane, manufacturing high-quality brass fittings, copper tubing, aluminium castings and the plaques for a post-war series of monuments instigated by the Deeside Field Club. A substantial three-storey and attic house in Crown Court was converted into office, finishing shop and pattern store while the stable became the foundry. Dr George Campbell, Professor of Divinity at Marischal College and principal from 1795–6 had a house in Crown Court, later leased by the General Dispensary, Vaccine and Lying-in Institution, from 1853. It could be that H & J Bryce were occupying this house, though in their day their backland premises were considered another possible home of the elusive Professor Beattie. The firm closed in 1967.

Next door to Crown Court was Charles Court. No involvement with Charles I or II has ever been established. You could walk through and arrive at the back of the Rubber Shop. The last was Burn Court, taking its name from the mill burn which to the north powered two dye works and the Tannery, as well as the flour mill across the road. All were demolished in 1977 and a largely unrecorded piece of Aberdeen's industrial history vanished. Now the former Upperkirkgate backlands are a loading area for the Bon Accord Centre.

CHAPTER 5

SCHOOLHILL
AND WOOLMANHILL

ST NICHOLAS KIRK

This detail from Parson Gordon's Plan of 1661 shows the 'Great Church' of St Nicholas still in its pre-Reformation architectural mode. The south transept, Drum's Aisle, is in front of the spire. The nave is left, the choir right. Gordon's

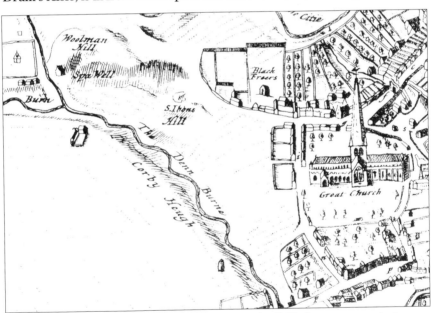

The Upperkirkgate (c), near top right, ran on into Schoolhill, the most convenient access to the great Mither Kirk of St Nicholas. The (g) on Parson Gordon's Plan, left of the steeple and indicating 'Schoolhill', is placed at a gap going straight into the kirkyard. George Jamesone's House is just above the (g). Corby Heugh, left, became Union Terrace Gardens and the 'pepperpot' below was the doocot of Doocot Brae, the site of today's 'Monkey House'. The Four Neukit Garden, enclosing the little barrel-vaulted house top left, was George Jamesone's gift to the town of his birth. To its right is Woolmanhill and the health-giving Spa Well, quite rural.

Plan also shows a tall building, 'Blackfreers', left of the church, once part of the Blackfriars' monastery which had survived the Reformation of a hundred years earlier. That has all passed away.

Two separate churches now occupy the space of the great Mither Kirk. The original, as shown by Parson Gordon, vanished at various times after the Reformation. Dedicated to the patron saint of the burgh, it was begun perhaps as early as 1060. As was the custom, the nave, the people's part of the kirk, lay to the west while in the east, beyond the crossing and the transepts, lay the most holy part of the building, the chancel or choir, which was sacred to the clergy. An ambitious scheme to build a truly magnificent choir was underway by the fifteenth century. Taxes were imposed on cargoes coming into harbour, the Common Good and other monies were earmarked for the 'Kirk Wark' and contributions of 'siller' (silver) and of salmon, and sheep-skins, precious church ornaments and vessels, and, usefully, lead, stone and lime, flowed in. St Nicholas, the largest parish church in Scotland, was a source of great local pride, and for some fifty years before the Reformation of 1560 enjoyed a golden age.

When word came that the 'rascal multitude' was on its way to loot the kirk in the name of the reformed religion, the town council stripped it of its treasures; they were not up for grabs. They had, after all, been gifted by countless townsfolk down the years. An armed guard was put on the kirk and the rabble driven off. Some years later the kirk's treasures were rouped for £46 sterling and the proceeds put towards repairs to the harbour and the Brig o' Balgownie; two cannons and ammunition were also purchased. Such was Aberdeen's way of dealing with the Reformation.

In 1596, when things had calmed down, St Nicholas was divided into two preaching kirks as approved by the reformed religion, the choir became the East Kirk, the nave the West. The latter had fallen into neglect by the 1730s and was not considered worth repairing. In 1746, the Duke of Cumberland, lodging in Aberdeen en route for Culloden, stored provender for his horses in the ruins. It was later decided to build a completely new West Kirk and James Gibbs, the renowned Aberdeen-born architect, then working in London, gifted the plans. It was completed in 1755, six years after Gibbs' death. This is the kirk we see today.

The East Kirk was pulled down in 1837. Archibald Simpson had insisted it was in a bad state of repair. It wasn't – the walls and arches were found to be sound. However the great man had drawn up plans for a new East Kirk in Gothic style and that was that. The original lead-covered spire remained, but crashed in the great fire of 1874, which also destroyed Simpson's relatively recent East Kirk. It was rebuilt in the same style by William Smith, John's son, who also designed a new spire. Again, this is the one we see today.

THE BLACKFRIARS
*

On the north side of Schoolhill, a little west of the kirk, were the spacious lands of the Blackfriars stretching back towards the Loch. King Alexander II established this order of preaching and teaching friars in Aberdeen in 1230, gifting them land which encompassed Schoolhill, Harriet Street, Crooked Lane, St Andrew's Street and Blackfriars Street. They built 'a very splendid monastery' where the 'Auld Hoose' (central block) of Robert Gordon's College now stands and ran a school on the site of the former Gray's School of Art. This could have been the origins of the Grammar School which gave Schoolhill its name. This would explain why the original location of the Grammar School was so far from the centre of the early town.

The Blackfriars enjoyed the protection of the magistrates and survived the Reformation relatively unscathed. Part of their property in Schoolhill passed to the Crown and thence to the Earl Marischal who put it towards his own pet educational project.

THE GRAMMAR SCHOOL
AND GORDON'S HOSPITAL
*

In spite of a possible early association with the Blackfriars, the Grammar School was taken under the wing of the magistrates from an early date in its long history, perhaps in the second half of the thirteenth century. By 1527 it was reported 'decayden and abill to fall down' and the master of kirkwork was instructed to repair it 'incontinent' (immediately). By 1589 it was to be repaired in 'thak' (thatch), and 'the vindois fixed' with 'the first and reddiest silver that they have or sall happin to ingett'. The town council was always short of ready money. Eleven years later the Grammar was 'presentlie ruinous and decaying' and £6 was disbursed towards its repair. In 1613, twenty-three shillings was put aside for repairs to the school, 'the thak thairof being blown off.' Ten years later it was neither 'wattertiicht' nor 'windticht'. It was rebuilt in 1626. By 1643 the overcrowding was such that a loft was put in. This may be the building in Parson Gordon's Plan to the right of 'Blackfreers'. It was still being thatched with 'heder' even by the late seventeenth century.

*The Auld Hoose, the original block of Robert Gordon's Hospital. As Fort Cumberland it
became the cantonment of the Hanoverian army before the march to Culloden in 1746.
It is certainly not lost, but its charming ogee pediments were replaced during the
extensions of 1830-33 by John Smith.*

At last, in 1757, a new Grammar School was built a short distance to the
west of its predecessor, even nearer to Blackfriars. This site was at the start
of an avenue that led to another new school building, the palatial Robert
Gordon's Hospital of 1739, now the Auld Hoose of Robert Gordon's College,
designed by William Adam at a cost of £3,000 from Robert Gordon's bequest.
The new Grammar in contrast was a plain single-storey, cottage-style building costing £400, from Patrick Dun's trust.

Gordon's Hospital had a far wider curriculum than the Grammar, where
Latin was the mainstay. Ironically, for all its splendour, Gordon's was a residential school for sons of poor burgesses who were to become apprentices,
while the Grammar was a day school attended by the sons of Aberdeen's
elite, many of whom went on to Marischal College. This was the school
young Geordie Gordon attended from 1795. The register for the summer term
of 1798 shows a line drawn through 'Geo B. Gordon' and 'Dom. de Byron'
written above. News of the death of his great-uncle had arrived in Broad
Street and the co-rector treated the new peer to cake and wine. Later that
summer the little pilgrim of eternity set out for Newstead Abbey.

As Gordon's Hospital expanded, the Grammar, 'a plain, dingy building',
became more rundown. The town council eventually took action and the

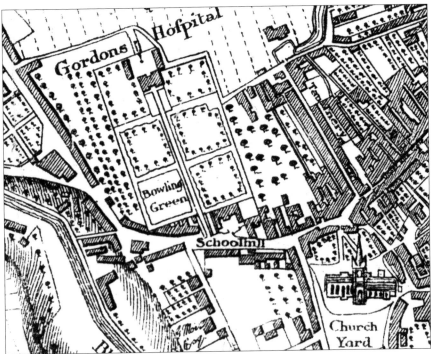

Taylor's Plan of 1773 shows the fertile gardens on the north side of Schoolhill, not yet built over. On 4 June 1779 the Aberdeen Journal *reported that 'ripe currants were gathered in a gentleman's garden in the Schoolhill'. The Mither Kirk was now the East and West Kirks of St Nicholas, and Gibbs' new West Kirk is on the left. 'Tannery', top right, was the future George Street. The Grammar School sits above the 'Schoolhill' sign. The south side of Schoolhill was built up with houses and shops in front of the kirkyard.*

The Grammar School in Lord Byron's day with a central block and two wings forming a three-sided square. Later, when two wings were added to the rear, it assumed an H shape. Junior pupils were taught in the front wings, seniors at the rear. The front range was the 'public school' where all pupils assembled.

school moved to its splendid new Scots baronial building in Skene Street in 1863. The old building was sold to the governors of Robert Gordon's College, as the Hospital now was, the following year. The east wing was rented out as offices and a warehouse, while the west became the Parochial Poors' Office. By the early 1880s, the school was being used as auxiliary classrooms for Gordon's, with the west wing rigged up as a chemistry lab. It was demolished in 1883 and the way was open for the redevelopment of Schoolhill.

SCHOOLHILL IN THE NINETEENTH CENTURY

GEORGE JAMESONE'S HOUSE

*

Strictly speaking, George Jamesone's House was Andrew Jamesone's own lodging, built by the master mason around 1586. Andrew had married into a gifted and prosperous extended family. His wife, Marjory Anderson, was sister of the mechanical genius Davie do a'thing, who was married to Dr William Guild's sister, and there was a double connection with the renowned medical and scientific Gregory family. Was Andrew advertising the quality of his work as well as providing a home for his young family? Why not? Other commissions followed, Provost Ross's House in the Shiprow for Robert Watson in 1587 and Mar's Castle, Gallowgate in 1595. The artist George Jamesone, second son of Andrew and Marjory, was born a year or so after the townhouse was completed. After studying at the Grammar School and Marischal College, both of which were about five minutes from the house, George travelled further afield, to Antwerp to sit with Van Dyck at the feet of Rubens, then to Italy. He returned to live in Aberdeen about 1625.

After the death of his elder brother, William, George inherited the Schoolhill mansion where he set up a studio. He moved to Edinburgh in 1635 and by the time of his death there in 1644 had painted most of Scotland's elite and was limner to Charles I, whose portrait he painted in 1633. There is an apocryphal tale that he offered it to the Aberdeen magistrates for hanging in the Town House but was so incensed by the niggardly sum they proposed to give him that he sold it to a stranger. Nevertheless he was philanthropically inclined, and 'out of his naturall affectioun to his native city' set up the Four Neukit Garden, Aberdeen's first public park, near the Well of Spa. Here he erected a timber barrel-vaulted house, which, Parson Gordon reported, he

William Garey's photograph of 1868 shows a Schoolhill that no longer exists. The first two houses on the right hand side, the premises of a vet and a plumber, had the traditional arcaded doors and windows. The sign, extreme right, announces the presence of Wordie & Co, carriers and agents for the Caledonian and North of Scotland railways whose stables were through the gap beside the cart laden with barrels. Next to that an inn, another building, then the famous George Jamesone's House.

'paynted all over with his own hand', just as his master Rubens had painted the inside and outside of his house in Antwerp. It has not survived.

George Jamesone's House, No. 12 Schoolhill, had many uses after Jamesone's day. It was occupied by a plumber, was a manse to St Nicholas Kirk, was John Hepburn's printing works, and in its twilight years, a common lodging house. By the 1880s Wordie & Co Ltd, the carriers, had acquired Jamesone's House and adjacent property for demolition in order to extend their stabling at Donald's Court which lay behind the north side of Schoolhill. By arrangement with the town council the new frontage was set back to allow the widening of Schoolhill. There was great public outrage at the demolition of George Jamesone's House in 1886 and the *Bon Accord* ran a cartoon entitled 'Vandals at Work' with lum-hatted business men tearing the place down. This was an early example of a business interest destroying an irreplaceable part of the townscape for its own benefit, with the approval of the council. It

R.W. Billings' drawing of Jamesone's House in the 1840s. Its great glory was a profusion of turrets. Both corners of the projecting front wing had corbelled round turrets at second floor level, and a stair turret was corbelled out from the first and to the second floors between the main house and the front wing. A little forecourt filled the gap between the main house and the front wing. Billings wrote enthusiastically of Aberdeen's turreted houses. Not one remains.

A sad-looking George Jamesone's House prior to demolition. The pepperpot roofs of the turrets, costly to maintain in a wind- and water-tight condition, were removed around 1850, robbing the building of its elegance. The forecourt has been boxed in. The usual attentive members of the public have gathered outside and across the narrow Schoolhill is the debris of houses that once backed onto St Nicholas Kirkyard.

would not be the last. Fortunately Messrs Matthews & Mackenzie, architects, created a handsome row of tenements at Nos 16–26 Schoolhill, the dormers echoing the turrets of George Jamesone's House. Almost the whole street was rebuilt at this time.

HARRIET STREET

✳

Harriet Street was a long, narrow lane between Schoolhill (opposite Back Wynd) and the western rump of Loch Street, 'little' Loch Street. Since the late nineteenth century a good part of the west side was occupied by Mitchell & Muil's bakery, the back regions of their handsome shop round in the upper part of Schoolhill. The lane was always choc-a-bloc with Mitchell & Muil vans, belching fumes, and folk queuing for yesterday's leftovers took their life in their hands. After the amalgamation of Strathdee and Mitchell & Muil as Sunblest Bakeries, the bakery in Harriet Street was surplus to requirements, and much of the west side of the lane was demolished and rebuilt as accommodation for the Robert Gordon University. The east side was knocked down to provide multi-storey parking for the Bon Accord Centre. Halfway along

Like the frontages of the Upperkirkgate, those of Schoolhill were exempted from the 'clean sweep' of 1986. However the building of a Boots the Chemist branch for the Bon Accord Centre necessitated reconstruction at the Harriet Street corner and the long-established J.W. Henderson, Ironmongers was replaced.

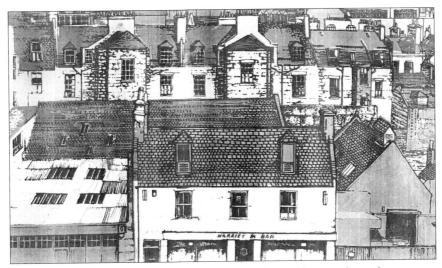

The Harriet Street Bar, with the houses of Donald's Court beyond.
Detail from a print by W. J. Watson.

the lane, the Harriet Street Bar (the Hairy Bar) a pleasant old traditional student pub was the last to go, and stood isolated for many months amidst scenes of devastation.

DONALD'S COURT
✳

Entered by a pend at No. 16 Schoolhill, the rectangular Donald's Court was bounded by Schoolhill, Harriet Street, 'little' Loch Street and George Street.

A fine segmental arch in Donald's Court prior to demolition.

141

The central portion was occupied by stabling for Wordie's horses and there were houses all around, including the once-handsome former Wordie office. Some of its residents had a touch of the exotic, such as the Pennys, who were photographers, a laundress, a jeweller and a painter. It could have made an ideal shopping mall, perhaps a courtyard surrounded by an arcade of shops and restaurants. It was demolished in 1987.

SOUTH SIDE
*

The south side of Schoolhill was demolished in 1885, a little earlier than the north side. On the bottom left-hand side of Garey's photograph (p.137), the future Reid & Pearson's site, the pestle and mortar symbol marked the premises of J. J. Urquhart, druggists. The next shop, tea and coffee merchants, was owned by the same family. Their business was taken over by the manager, Thomas Curr. He set up his well-known Curr's Coffee business on the other side of the road when the great upheaval was over. The next group of houses backed onto St Nicholas's kirkyard. The little white house was that of Burnett Carr the gravedigger. Legend has it that it was into one of those houses that Dr Andrew Moir the anatomist fled in December 1831 when escaping the mob

Demolition of the houses backing onto the St Nicholas graveyard in 1885.
The little house of the gravedigger is centre. Across the road, a turret of
George Jamesone's House still stands.

who had invaded his St Andrew Street 'burkin hoose' and were now in hot pursuit. He jumped out of the back window, landing in the graveyard, where he hid, not daring to return to his home in the Guestrow until night fell.

The house at the top left-hand side of Garey's photograph is James Dun's House, 1769. Dun was headmaster of the Grammar School, located opposite, in Byron's time. After a number of genteel residents, it became an annexe to the old Central School (Aberdeen Academy), deteriorated badly, but was reconstructed as a little civic museum opening in 1975. It was in part an exercise to show councillors how successfully derelict buildings could be restored. It later fell foul of 'cutbacks', was closed, sold and became a beauty parlour in 2004: not quite lost but certainly curiously metamorphosed. The gable-end beyond belonged to a house which was demolished to make way for the Central School, now a shopping mall. Out of sight is Belmont Street, then the brick spire of the Triple Kirks, now partly ruinous. Mutton Brae lay below.

MUTTON BRAE

*

Mutton Brae was a hamlet of red pantiled 'hoosies' which sprang up in a haphazard fashion on the brae below the north-west end of Belmont Street, though to be accurate, the 'Brae' was in existence before Belmont. A site for the first house 'upon that piece of ground lying on the south side of Schoolhill' was granted to George Smith, blacksmith in 1749, while Belmont Street did not begin to be feued out until 1774. The two communities were like chalk and cheese. Belmont's generous building stances found favour with the gentry, while William Smith, writing in 1902, years after they had vanished, recalled that the houses of Mutton Brae:

> Sat about in a higgledy-piggledy manner, as if they had been built in the Schoolhill and then slid down the brae to settle as chance happened. They were all shapes and sizes, gable-ends and outside stairs being their most conspicuous features. The cluster of modest dwellings on that breakneck brae had a most picturesque appearance.

The layout was not totally chaotic. There was a Back Brae, a Middle Brae and a Front Brae where 'the better class of tradesman lived'. Mrs Mary Hall who came in from the country kept a byre and kye on the Front Brae and provided milk and butter for the Mutton Brae folk for years. It was a friendly place, with summer evenings spent across at the Corby Well with the women knit-

The Triple Kirks tower above the houses of Mutton Brae. The Denburn flows through the middle of the picture towards Union Bridge and local people gather at the public bleach green. Corby Heugh is extreme right.

ting their 'shanks', or with soirees in the brick-floored kitchens where a fiddler would play. Many were employed at the Schoolhill Factory, a hand-loom weaving shed run by Gordon Barron & Co which was closed in 1830. In 1843 the lawyer Francis Edmond acquired the derelict building in anticipation of the Disruption. It was demolished and Archibald Simpson built the Triple Kirks, partly from the factory down-takings. This was the beginning of the end for Mutton Brae, for houses at the top were demolished to make way for the Kirks.

Twenty or so years later, the lower houses were demolished. They lay in the path of the new Denburn Valley Junction Railway, now the main line to Inverness, where it runs alongside Union Terrace Gardens. The end of

Mutton Brae came twenty years later. By 1885 the Town Council had built the upper section of a new access to Rosemount, later named Rosemount Viaduct, which ran from Union Terrace across Skene Street, to the foot of South Mount Street. A lower section would now run from the west end of Schoolhill to join Union Terrace. To carry this out it was necessary to create the Denburn Viaduct (sometimes called the Schoolhill Viaduct) to bridge the Denburn Valley. In August 1885, the remaining houses in Mutton Brae were purchased by the council for demolition. The remaining inhabitants, pawnbrokers and chimney sweeps went their separate ways and the little community was finally disbanded.

WOOLMANHILL

We can cross now to Woolmanhill, the place of the ancient Aberdeen wool-market, which was out of town in Parson Gordon's time. An early infirmary was built here in 1741, beside the healing waters of the Spa Well, but was demolished and replaced by Archibald Simpson's splendid building of the 1830s. Just east of the hospital was an unpromising triangular piece of common land, 'whereon the middens are laid', but by the nineteenth century, it was mostly built up.

JOSEPH ROBERTSON
*

One of Aberdeen's finest historians, Joseph Robertson, was born in 1810 at No. 37 Woolmanhill. His father, who had a general merchant's shop there, died when he was only seven, but his widowed mother managed to provide him with the best education Aberdeen could offer. He was educated at the Grammar School and Marischal College, where his days were not altogether uneventful. The mob who regularly hounded Dr Andrew Moir recognised a medical student leaving the quad in company, as it chanced, with Robertson. They were pelted with dead hens, chased into the Guestrow and had their hats destroyed.

Robertson became a law apprentice and freelance journalist and had a precocious interest in local history. By 1831, at the age of twenty-one, he had written a *Guide to the Highlands of Deeside*. When furthering his career in Edinburgh in 1839 he found time to write the first (and only) volume of the remarkable *Book of Bon Accord*, the city's most erudite and readable history, other than Alexander Keith's. He was only twenty-nine. Back in Aberdeen he became a founder of the Spalding Club and edited several of the early publications. He also edited newspapers in Edinburgh and Glasgow and in 1852 was appointed Curator of the Historical Department at HM Register House, Edinburgh, whose University later honoured him with an LL.D. Meanwhile his *Guide to the Highlands* had gone through fifteen editions. It caused much surprise when Robertson was revealed as its author in 1869, three years after his death. Everyone thought it had been written by James Brown, the Ballater coachman, but Robertson had thought it a good wheeze to borrow his name as a *nom de plume*.

THE WOOLMANHILL TRIANGLE

*

The south end of Woolmanhill formed part of a distinctive triangle that had St Andrew Street at its base, Woolmanhill at the west and Blackfriars Street at the east. The apex extended almost to Schoolhill but the buildings there, along with the Blackfriars Street corner, were demolished to make way for the Cowdray Hall and the War Memorial.

The west side of Blackfriars Street looked like back premises, with few entrances or windows. For many years Robert Meff had a yeast business there in an old building, its rickety wooden floors covered with sacks. On the Woolmanhill side itself were two well-known firms, Robert Whitelaw, surgical instrument makers and J. Stephen & Sons, a long-established picture-frame maker whose workshops were nearby in Rodgers Walk. By the early

Woolmanhill in the 1870s, looking towards Schoolhill and the Triple Kirks.
The apex of the triangle ends with the lower houses, centre, while the tall building
beyond belongs to the Blackfriars Street corner.

Demolition is beginning c. 1920 on the east side of Blackfrairs Street which had been laid out in the late eighteenth century on the old monastery garden of the Blackfriars. The Art Gallery, glimpsed extreme right, opened in 1884.

The handsome Accident and Emergency Building, completed in 1912, stood opposite the Infirmary, in the block immediately north of the triangle. It has been replaced by a roundabout.

twentieth century the business was flourishing with tons of mouldings arriving at Woolmanhill on a regular basis and Mr James Stephen visiting Germany and the USA to seek out the latest in designs. Here too were Pole, Silver & Coutts, warehousemen, and a firm of funeral undertakers with the usual flower urn in the window. British Paints Ltd had an extensive though old building with plain wooden floors. They would mix paints for customers in the basement. An electrician was based there from at least the 1920s and there was a second-hand bookshop where you could exchange magazines. An Army Training Centre occupied the base of the triangle, opposite North St Andrew Street. The triangle vanished piecemeal and lies under the Denburn dual carriageway. Once so familiar, it is now hard to remember exactly where it was.

BLACK'S BUILDINGS
*

Blacks' Buildings, a small curving crescent of tall tenements, four and five storeys high, sat below the Royal Infirmary, Woolmanhill, just west of the apex of the Woolmanhill triangle. Their back greens invaded the north end of the Corby Heugh. The houses were built in stages between 1789 and 1830, by the wine merchant James Black, who lived at Willowbank House and carried on his business at Crown Court where No. 41½ Union Street now stands. The front doors had attractive fanlights, while the rear elevation had high gables, stepped slated roofs and, near the south end, a projecting semi-circular stair tower. Black was involved in numerous disputes with the police commissioners, the traffic authority of the day, one bone of contention being the construction of the westerly tenement of his 'crescent', directly in the line of Skene Street as shown in Beattie's plan on p.148.

Left. Plan for the proposed Denburn Gardens (which became Union Terrace Gardens), drawn by the surveyor James Hay Beattie in 1869. The Gardens did not quite take this shape, but the positions of the buildings are accurate. Woolmanhill Infirmary is top right and Black's Buildings, with washing greens at the back, curve below. The bent and pointed end of Skene Street is to the left. The Denburn Viaduct has not yet been built and there is no Schoolhill Station or His Majesty's Theatre. Below Black's Buildings, right, is the apex of the triangle of buildings between Woolmanhill, left, and the tall buildings of Blackfriars Street, right, which turn the corner to the site of the future Art Gallery. Denburn Terrace, including one very tall house, is left of the Gardens, and on the extreme left is Union Terrace. Woolmanhill Infirmary is the only building still extant if we discount the Triple Kirks, below, then in their heyday.

*Black's Buildings, centre, looking more or less immaculate before the building of the
Denburn Viaduct. The pediment of the Royal Infirmary, Woolmanhill is in the distance
and in the foreground, the footbridge crossing the Corby Heugh/Union Terrace Gardens.*

Collie's Brig Warehouse, more formally Morrison's Economic Stores,
which operated from the basement of the westerly tenement, was established
in 1863 by Miss J. Morrison. It took its nickname from a little stone bridge,
built in 1802, across the Denburn, where it ran in the open near the foot of
Skene Street. Another nickname for the Stores, which were reached by stone
steps, was 'The Hole'. In 1886, this part of Black's Buildings caught fire and
the Stores, with Miss Morrison's brother now in charge, moved to the
Netherkirkgate where it gained its most famous nickname yet, 'Raggy'
Morrison's.

Black's Buildings, once tenements of quality, became dilapidated, grimy
with engine smoke after the coming of the railway, and acquired an evil reputation as Aberdeen's most infamous slums. In 1925 there were complaints that
they should have been demolished years earlier. These tenements had some
character in their early days, but restoration was not an option. They were
pulled down in 1957. Skene Street could at last be straightened to run in a
direct line to Woolmanhill.

SCHOOLHILL STATION

*

When the new road to link Schoolhill and Union Terrace, the future Denburn Viaduct, was proposed the managers of the Great North of Scotland Railway (GNSR) saw the advantage of locating a station in the vicinity to serve their Aberdeen – Dyce suburban route. Negotiations followed with the Town Council's Improvements Committee who agreed to alter the width of the proposed viaduct's spans and to sell ground east and west of the railway line to accommodate the new station. Even though it would be largely below road level, workmanship was to be of the same high standard as the viaduct. The hewn work and face-work on the new buildings were respectively, of the finest Kemnay and Rubislaw granites.

Work on Schoolhill Station (officially in Rosemount Viaduct), began in the autumn of 1890. The design was unusual. A thirty-three-feet gangway gave access from the pavement to the top floor of a three-storey square tower. Passengers would then descend by stairs to a booking hall on the second floor and a general and ladies' waiting rooms at platform level. The gangway was intended to be covered and a second overhead gangway was proposed for the

Schoolhill Station during its days as a café. His Majesty's Theatre rises behind and the Royal Infirmary, Woolmanhill is to the extreme right. Black's Buildings, prior to demolition in 1957, are to the right of the station. The ornate railings, foreground, were salvaged from the footbridge across the north end of Union Terrace Gardens.

convenience of passengers using the up line, with an entrance from the Denburn Road. The station opened a little behind schedule in 1893 and these additions never appeared. By 1894 the suburban line handily linked Dyce with Culter via Aberdeen Joint. It served a wide clientele: millworkers living in the east end who worked at Woodside or Stoneywood, as well as Robert Gordon's pupils who could board the train at their West Cults' back gardens and dismount a stone's throw from school. His Majesty's Theatre was in business next door from 1906, and scenery, props and costume baskets were offloaded from goods carriages direct to the rear of the theatre.

By the 1930s, the GNSR's subbie line was running at considerable loss, the result of direct competition from Alexanders Buses. Services were discontinued in April 1937 and fourteen stations closed, including Schoolhill. The station later became a café which, like the old GNSR passengers, one entered via the gangway on the viaduct. The station was demolished in 1975, leaving as its only momento, blocks of rustic granite in the viaduct which marked the access to the gangway. During 2004–5 a glass extension to His Majesty's Theatre was built alongside the old site.

PART 2
Granite City
*

A city with an entrance at last! Union Bridge, c. 1835, showing the original width of 40ft as decreed by Thomas Telford. Archibald Simpson's powerful Aberdeen Hotel, centre, is still extant, though no longer a hotel. Extreme left, Lumsden of Belhelvie's townhouse on the Union Street/Terrace corner, later replaced by the Monkey House. Right, a glimpse of the buildings that preceded Trinity Hall Mark II.

CHAPTER 6

AROUND UNION STREET
AND THE NEW MARKET

INTRODUCTION

*

Union Street had a difficult birth. It bankrupted the city and continues to be a problem. It all began in the 1790s when Charles Abercrombie, the Glasgow surveyor working on the new turnpike road system for the County of Aberdeen, rose to a challenge from the city's magistrates. He would 'render more convenient not only the approach into your town' – the old Hardgate, Green, Bow Brig route was still the only one – but in a manner that would improve 'the general prosperity of your city'. However the approved scheme for a new street that would 'open up' the town was not Abercrombie's brainchild, but that of a woolcomber in Provost Ley's employment, so it is said, whose rough drafts were passed to the surveyor. It was a plan for a thoroughfare that would link the proposed turnpike routes from Inverurie at St Nicholas Street and from the north at the future King Street; from the south and from Skene at what became Holburn Junction. It would run from the Castlegate but initially only as far west as the Summer Road (Summer Street), where it would link with the Hardgate.

Named Union Street to commemorate the union of Great Britain and Ireland in 1801, this new thoroughfare was to be built as a viaduct or flyover. A number of hurdles had to be overcome: St Catherine's Hill (north face removed); the Valley of the Denburn (bridged); properties, mainly cottages, on the intended line (bought and demolished); lack of funding (borrowed). The new road was built above unpromising terrain by a series of 'blind' brick arches still visible at Carnegie's Brae, Correction Wynd and behind the Back Wynd Stairs. By the time today's Diamond Street was reached, the ground had levelled and a great plain stretched westward.

UNION BRIDGE

*

All construction was manual and the most demanding task was the engi-
neering of a great bridge across the Denburn Valley, the great chasm now
occupied by the railway line and Union Terrace Gardens. This project got off
to a faulty start, but Thomas Fletcher, the engineer who had been working on
the Aberdeenshire Canal, saved the day with a design for a single-span
bridge. Work began in earnest in 1802. Fletcher's elegant, well-proportioned
'Grand Arch' took shape, embellished with a stone parapet and balustrade of
highly dressed granite by James Burn of Haddington who was conveniently
designing the Aberdeen Bank at the top of Marischal Street at this time. Burn
simply repeated his fine parapet from the roof of the bank. At last, on 23
February 1805, the *Aberdeen Journal* reported that 'a gentleman on horseback
passed along the line of Union Street and crossed the Grand Arch over the

The Denburn Valley in 1807 looking south to Union Bridge, most spectacular when
viewed from below, with the old Bow Brig beyond, from Carr's Caledonian Sketches.
The Denburn flows on the left, the path extreme left, the Denburnside, is now the
Denburn dual carriageway. The Corby Heugh extreme right and the public
bleach green adjoining it later formed Union Terrace Gardens.

Denburn on his way out of town'. Union Bridge, its single span the largest in Scotland at that time, ranked in importance with Edinburgh's North Bridge.

Lord Medwyn's aphorism, quoted at the beginning of this book, may now be revealed in its entirety. Aberdeen had been 'a city without an entrance'; now it was 'an entrance without a city'. The Grand Arch was the new entrance, but the gentleman on his way out of town in 1805 was riding along a street that stretched as far as the eye could see, with not, as yet, a building in sight.

Today Union Bridge, though physically still there, has gone missing. Fletcher had proposed increasing its width from the original 60 feet to 70 feet, but Thomas Telford, the consultant, was adamant that it be reduced to 40 feet, making a clear statement that it was a bridge, not merely part of the street and not to be abutted with houses. For the next hundred years there were complaints that it was far too narrow, and indeed with the coming of trams the journalist William Carnie joked that it seemed to be contracting. Widening to 60 feet eventually took place in 1908 and the original Georgian Bridge vanished from sight, obscured by steel arches and girders.

Union Bridge around 1815. A few buildings have at last begun to appear.
On the left, on the corner with Union Terrace is Lumsden of Belhelvie's townhouse,
demolished 1885, perhaps the earliest residence. The pantiled cottages of Windmill
Brae in the foreground have not yet yielded to progress.

UNION TERRACE

We can look now at Union Terrace, which grew concurrently with Union Bridge and which puts the finishing touches on the Woolmanhill story. It was a sought-after area with building stances snapped up even before the ground was levelled. The original buildings, nearly all now lost, were plain-fronted and restrained. One exception, at the junction with Union Street, was No. 1 Union Terrace, the combined winter residence and legal chambers of Harry Lumsden of Belhelvie, laird, businessman and advocate in Aberdeen. The townhouse was not ornate but it was grand in scope, curving with the Terrace and with a turreted stair block placed well forward on the corner. It latterly became the Northern Club, before it became Royal and flitted west. The other buildings enjoyed a mix of commercial and residential occupants: lawyers; doctors; ministers; ironmongers; Peter Cleland, an artist, at No. 8; clerks; teachers; a shuttle maker, and lodgings. By the end of the nineteenth century, edifices of varying degrees of magnificence had replaced several of the original buildings. Most splendid of all was A. Marshall Mackenzie's

headquarters for the Northern Assurance Company, which by 1885 had replaced Lumsden of Belhelvie's townhouse. From 1968 it became the Commercial Union offices and latterly, General Accident. It was nicknamed the 'Monkey House', and became the Monkey House bar in 2004.

BON ACCORD FREE CHURCH
*

The other exception to the plain-fronted houses was the roughly triangular Bon Accord Church at the north end. It started out in 1823 as Union Terrace Chapel and five years later was acquired by a section of the congregation that had split from Trinity Church at the old Trinity Friars Place. They called a minister of their own choosing, the redoubtable Gavin Parker. In the summer of 1843, with his flock solidly behind him, Parker came 'out' at the Disruption, and held open-air services across in the Corby Heugh. The kirk was eventually rouped and bought at the upset price by a member of the congregation to serve as the new Free Church.

Union Terrace in 1890. Only the 'Monkey House', extreme left, is recognisable.

Bon Accord Free Church, Union Terrace. It remained in the Terrace until 1896.

MANN'S GRAND AND KELLY'S BANK
✳

By 1893, offices and a detective agency at Nos 10–13 in mid-terrace, were replaced by Charles Mann's splendid Grand Hotel, with its handsome flight of steps at the entrance and elaborate plasterwork. Mann's rivals advertised that the Palace Hotel was in the station because of its linking walkway, so Mann retaliated by advertising that the Grand was in Union Terrace Gardens. It became the Caledonian in 1930, later a Thistle Hotel, and was acquired by Atlantic Hotels in 2003. The hotel took over No. 14, a neighbouring, plain-fronted building, in the 1950s and its original detailing was removed. In spite of these shortcomings it was very popular as Aberdeen's first cocktail bar, the Copper Kettle. It was in the 1950s too that Nos 17 and 18 Union Terrace, set back from the road and next but one to the Bon Accord Church, were demolished and replaced by a bland modern structure as an extension for the Trustee Savings Bank next door at No. 19. This bank was a very different kettle of fish. Built in 1895 on the Union Terrace-Diamond

Place corner in Italian Renaissance style as the head office of Aberdeen Savings Bank, No. 19 was Dr William Kelly's finest work. His meticulous craftsmanship and attention to detail rivalled that of Charles Rennie McIntosh.

THE OLD COUNTY BUILDINGS
*

In 1896 Bon Accord Free Church moved to an impressive suite of church buildings in the newly completed Rosemount Viaduct, where it remains today. To finance the move, the Kirk sold its Union Terrace building as a site for the new School Board Buildings, which became part of the glorious triumvirate, Nos 20 -25, erected in Renaissance style in harmony with Kelly's Bank, and later known as the Old County Buildings. Nos 20 and 22, by A. Marshall Mackenzie, were erected in 1897 for the Aberdeen Parish Council and Aberdeen School Board respectively. No. 25, by A.G. Sydney Mitchell & Wilson, dates from 1902 and was originally designed for the Scottish Life

Union Terrace c. 1900. From left, a couple of plain originals, Kelly's Bank and the Parish and School Board Buildings. No. 25 has not yet been built and a shop with house above is on the site.

*Two masterpieces by A. Marshall Mackenzie, left, the Northern Assurance Co.
headquarters (the Monkey House) and right, the grand Hotel for Charles Mann,
flank two sets of plain fronted buildings.*

Assurance Company. The group has been handsomely restored as commercial offices. Towards the end of the terrace are four early nineteenth-century
tenements. They became run down, but were attractively modernised by the
Aberdeen District Council in the mid-1970s.

Two sets of plain-fronted buildings next door to the 'Monkey House'
were the offices of lawyers, accountants and coal merchants. A cheery fire
was always burning at Ellis & McHardy's. Miss Alice Copeland, stenogra-
pher, was at No. 5, and Jean Forrest, hairdresser at No. 9 for many years. The
taller block, inspired by its grander neighbours, acquired an ornate frontage.
Both blocks were demolished and replaced in 1979 by a Lloyds Bank, an evil-
looking structure with a curious box on top. The Lloyds TSB merger has
affected the Terrace and Kelly's wondrous building at No. 19 is closed to
customers and the little lepard faces of its down pipe sport an unhealthy
coating of green slime.

A second set, Nos 15 and 16, date from the early nineteenth century, and

*The taller of the two plain buildings opposite, inspired by the
Caledonian Hotel (Mann's Grand until 1930), now sports an ornate frontage.
Both were replaced by Lloyds Bank.*

were the last to retain their original plain fronts. Both have been atractively
refurbished. No. 15 was the townhouse of the Farquharsons of Whitehouse,
where the family had its law offices and where Mrs Peter Farquharson gave
much talked of parties. From 1915 when it was founded until the 1990s, No.
15 housed Aberdeen Chamber of Commerce and has a fine door-case inserted
into the original opening. No. 16, though altered to its detriment, retains an
extra-large cartwheel fanlight over the transom.

UNION TERRACE GARDENS
*

No houses were planned for the east side of Union Terrace where the upper
part of the Corby Heugh, still undeveloped, had an irregular shape, making
curves in the terrace. The trees were separated from the pavement by an iron
railing 'rendered conspicuous', Robert Anderson tells us, 'latterly by the

Union Terrace Gardens evolving out of the old Corby Heugh before Rosemount Viaduct was built. Behind the bandstand the iron footbridge crosses between Mutton Brae (not shown) and Denburn Terrace, left. The lost houses of Skene Terrace are in the centre, back, at right angles to those of Denburn Terrace.

absence of the spikes, most of which were maliciously removed', doubtless by mid-nineteenth-century vandals. By 1877 the council took up an earlier proposal of Councillor James Matthews, architect, future lord provost and champion of the area, to convert Corby Heugh's wooded bank and adjoining bleachfield into a pleasure park. Neglected trees were thinned out, new foliage introduced and the ground was carefully sloped and planted out and the bleach green moved further north. Union Terrace Gardens was taking shape. A light, iron footbridge with a handsome wrought-iron parapet was slung across the Denburn Valley Railway line to take pedestrians from Woolmanhill, Schoolhill and the remnants of the Mutton Brae community across to Denburn Terrace and Union Terrace, and the Gardens were enhanced by a splendid bandstand.

The linking of Schoolhill and Union Terrace in 1885, as well as chopping off the north-easterly end of Skene Terrace (it now starts at No. 40) brought

Left and top right. The Union Terrace Gardens Gents'.

Below right. The Union Terrace Gardens Ladies'.

about the end of Denburn Terrace a pleasant-looking street of houses in the vernacular, some with fanlights. It was replaced by the spur street, which curves gracefully between the statues of Prince Albert and William Wallace. With the Woolmanhill/Schoolhill area now linked by the Denburn Viaduct and the lower end of Rosemount Viaduct, the iron footbridge was declared superfluous and dismantled

Union Terrace was extended by constructing arches in the Gardens and building out over them. In the 1890s the council narrowly voted in favour of providing ladies' and gents' toilets in the Gardens, under the arches nearest the south-west entrance. Thus came about the superb Victorian toilets of which Aberdonians were proud, with their stained-glass windows, beauti-fully tiled walls and inlaid mosaic floors. Spotless, carbolic-scented, with a unique clicking and clacking of shoes going over the glazed trapdoors set in the pavement above, they were always memorable. Although a civic amenity, they were latterly poorly looked after, vandalised not only by ordinary vandals but also in the crass manner of their maintenance. Though most towns would have been proud to have them, they were closed down c. 2000.

The Union Terrace Gardens bandstand. It was removed many years ago.
By J.A. Sutherland.

UNION STREET

It took many years before Union Street was fully lined with buildings. Feus were expensive and anticipated revenue from their sale was slow to materialise. High standards were demanded. It was conceded that different purchasers would have different ideas. Variety would be allowed, provided it did not compromise 'the Uniformity and Regularity of the Street'. 'The Houses between each opening or Cross Street should form one Compartment, and be of the same height, number of Floors and pitch of Roof.' Between Union Bridge and the Castlegate the permitted height was four storeys, the finish, highly dressed granite.

What emerged was a street that was cool, classical, elegant and chic, with breath-taking symmetry, which retained the tradition of stylish arcading. As Fenton Wyness wrote in *More Spots from the Leopard* of the two great architects of Union Street:

> The scholarly work of John Smith and Archibald Simpson in adapting Classic forms – the vogue being Grecian – to buildings of their own time was a remarkable achievement, while the effects they obtained by using the hard crystalline granite can only be described as masterly.

Though the creation of Union Street liberated the city from its medieval corset, only the rich could afford to live there. (It also *inter alia* plunged the

This curve-ended 1820s block between the Correction Wynd Stairs at the former Gloucester Hotel building and St Nicholas Street was an admirable example of the 'compartment'. Centre, the Commercial Bank, No. 78 Union Street, rounded off this block at the east end. Extreme right on the other side of St Nicholas Street is the Town & County Bank, now the Clydesdale Bank.

city into bankruptcy in 1817 though the debt was cleared by 1825.) In the second half of the nineteenth century the character of the street began to change. A few original buildings were lost, though they were not replaced by anything shoddy, but by the grandiose new architecture of Aberdeen Triumphant. The city was booming and the new head offices of banks and assurance companies reflected this confidence. Confident, triumphant Aberdeen had already made its mark in and around the Castlegate area, with the North Bank, 1842, the Municipal Buildings, 1867, the Salvation Army Citadel, 1893 and the spectacular Gaudi-in-granite Marischal College frontage, 1903. The movement spread into Union Street with the stylish Trinity Hall Mark Two, John & William Smith, 1846, for the Seven Incorporated Trades, on the south-east corner of Union Bridge, replacing original buildings. The ornate and elegant headquarters of Town & County Bank of 1862, now the Clydesdale St Nicholas Branch, had replaced original buildings, as had the handsome Nos 26–30 Union Street (Ellis & Wilson) for the *Aberdeen Free Press* in 1887. Across St Catherine's Wynd (Nos 32–38), Alexander Ellis was reaching for the stars in 1897 with his magnificent edifice for Sangster & Henderson, drapers and house furnishers.

UNION STREET WEST
*

Union Street was laid out only as far as the Summer Road (Summer Street). The area from Union Bridge to Summer Street (north side) and to Bon Accord Terrace (south side, linking with the Hardgate) was initially known as Union Street West.

Union Street West. The immaculate block between Gilcomston Kirk at Summer Street and Union Row, just out of view, right, in the 1890s. The west end of Union Street was favoured as a residential area by the professional classes.

La Scala shortly before demolition in 1935. The domestic aspect of
Union Street West is still evident in the dormers.

The Gilcomston Kirk – Union Row block was altered by the appearance
of La Scala, Aberdeen's first custom-built cinema in 1914 at No. 234, and its
slightly earlier neighbour, the pedimented, beautifully balanced Clydesdale
Bank at No. 232 at the corner of Union Row. More changes followed in the
1920s when T. Scott Sutherland, architect and town councillor, bought the
house of the distinguished surgeon, Sir Alexander Ogston, at No. 252 and
subsequently acquired that of his neighbour Dr R.A. Galloway at No. 250.
Here Sutherland created a restrained art deco office block in 1934 for the
Scottish Amicable Building Society. In 1936 he replaced La Scala with his
finest picture house, the Majestic.

UNION PLACE
*

Union Place developed independently along the stretch between Summer
Street/Bon Accord Terrace, and Holburn Junction. This was largely a residential quarter, its spacious houses favoured, like Union Street West, by
doctors and lawyers. In 1890 the town council decreed that the whole area
become Union Street, though this did not go down well with residents.

Union Place looking west. Babbie Law retired from her licensed shop, top left, in 1885, and it was later replaced by a bank. She had given her name to Hoburn Junction, though it is not heard now. The imposing building on the extreme right was first the Water House, from 1886 a branch of William Bain's carriage hire empire, and for many years, a bank.

Traces of the old houses are still evident and even now the former Union Place has a different character from the rest of Union Street.

THE PALACE BUILDINGS
*

At the end of the '30s the Granite City tradition remained intact. Union Street was still recognisable as a gracious Georgian thoroughfare, though peppered with exuberant Victorian outbursts and dashes of a subdued though distinctive art deco, of which the superb Capitol Cinema (A. Marshall Mackenzie & Son and Clement George, 1932–4) and the Burton building (presently Top Shop) at the top of Market Street (George Watt, 1929) are examples. The curve-ended Correction Wynd Stairs-St Nicholas Street block lost its symmetry in 1928 when the Commercial Bank at the St Nicholas Street corner was demolished and replaced in 1936 by the National Commercial Bank (Jenkins & Marr), now the Royal Bank, which immediately engaged in an acroteria war with Burton's opposite. But the new bank was so overwhelmingly splendid that who could suspect warning shots?

So when did Union Street start to lose its style? Aberdonians will argue about this but I date it back to the time that the former Palace Hotel site was under negotiation. It all began in 1873 when the prestigious south-west corner site of Union Bridge was acquired by John Keith of the drapers Pratt & Keith, to erect a splendid edifice, the Palace Buildings, to accommodate the firm's expanding business. Pratt & Keith with their tenant, James Lorimer, bootmaker, occupied the lower floors and the architect, James Matthews, suggested successfully that instead of giving over the remaining space to office and residential accommodation as planned, he create a first-class hotel. Thus the Palace Hotel came into being.

Palace Buildings shortly after completion, with the Aberdeen turret trademark. They would have balanced Lumsden of Belhelvie's townhouse on the Union Terrace corner. John Smith's magnificent Trinity Hall is left and Union Bridge still has a south side.

The Palace Buildings were acquired by the Great North of Scotland Railway in 1891 and the lessee of the Palace Hotel, Charles Mann, in a huff, went off to run his own show in Union Terrace, at 'Mann's Grand', later the Caledonian Hotel. The GNSR embarked on an ambitious programme of refurbishment and added an additional floor, thus altering the appearance from Scots baronial to Victorian railway hotel and in a sell-and-lease-back agreement Pratt & Keith now became tenants. The 'Palace', which had its own subway link with Aberdeen Joint Station, enjoyed a reputation as hoteliers to the great and the good. The end came in 1941 when the building was destroyed by fire, claiming the lives of six female members of staff who were asleep in the top-storey bedrooms at the time of the outbreak. It stood, a gaunt ruin, sometimes mistaken for bomb damage, until 1950 when the site was at last cleared.

THE 'SHARGAR SHOPPIES'

*

A new building for C&A Modes went up on the Palace site in 1957 though the Dutch firm was not permitted to display its rainbow logo, planners considering it inappropriate to the *dignitas* of Union Street. Meanwhile the developers who were carrying out negotiations for the new building spotted the air space above the south side of Union Bridge between the old Palace Hotel/C&A site and Trinity Hall. Here was a 'gap site' ripe for development – and it was perhaps here that the rot set in. In the late 1950s planning permission was granted to develop the air space and in 1963, a row of prefabricated shops resembling two-storey portacabins was slung across the south side of the bridge, obliterating the view across the railway to Torry. That was the final nail in the coffin of Union Bridge as Grand Arch. Stand on the Denburn Viaduct today and look south, and you may make out a drab steel arch, dominated by shops above and topped by a clutter of box-like constructions.

The poet Alexander Scott, was prompted to write of his fellow Aberdonians:

Bonnieness-blind, thae fowk fir a their birr!
Wha else i the stanie straucht o Union Street,
Wi only the ae brig till open space,
Wad block thon brichtness out wi shargar shoppies?

The south side of Union Bridge, an evocative view painted just after the war by the artist Dan Stephen.

This is unfair, for the scheme was carried out in the face of considerable public hostility. In its defence, John M. Graham, professor of Systematic Theology and lord provost at the time, argued that it would be good for the rates. Other developers, inspired by this breath-taking entrepreneurism, sought permission to carry out parallel schemes on the north side of the bridge in the 1960s. This proposed desecration, the blocking out of the view across to His Majesty's Theatre, was too much even for the most bonnieness-blind, rates-orientated councillor and the plans came to nought.

CRIMONMOGATE'S HOUSE
*

The coming of the 'shargar shoppies' sent out a message to predatory developers and for years after it was open season on Union Street. We can start with the Music Hall. Archibald Simpson's Assembly Rooms of 1822 had been expanded to the rear by Matthews' Music Hall of 1859. By 1961 the place had been allowed to deteriorate, the interior featuring all-in-wrestling and sales

From left, Crimonmogate's House (the Royal Northern Club) and Provost Anderson's townhouse (the YMCA), both demolished in 1963, and the Music Hall.

of work, the entrance hall and central corridor littered with milk crates and tacky chairs. An Edinburgh development company wanted to demolish it as part of a redevelopment scheme. To the rescue came Sir Alexander Gibson and Sir John Barbirolli. Gibson pointed out that many a continental orchestra would be pleased to have a hall half the size of the Music Hall. Barbirolli echoed him, adding, please tell the people of Aberdeen not to allow the sacrilege of having this place destroyed.

Rebuffed but undeterred, the would-be developers persevered and succeeded with the Royal Northern Club at No. 204 Union Street, on the east corner of Huntly Street, whose members had by then moved to Albyn Place. Built originally by John Smith in 1810 for Peter Milne of Crimonmogate, it was the first townhouse to go up west of Union Bridge. With its elegant Tuscan columns, it was, wrote Edward Meldrum, 'one of the most attractive buildings of real architectural merit on Aberdeen's main thoroughfare'. The Music Hall a little to the east was grander, but in perfect harmony with Crimonmogate's House whose tall, elegant neighbour, a former townhouse of the entrepreneurial provost Sir Alexander Anderson, latterly a YMCA, was

The south-east side of Union Street in the 1860s with its symmetry virtually intact.
Extreme right, the Palace Hotel, the south side of Union Bridge with a view down to the
houses of Denburn Road with Hadden's Mill looming in the background. All gone.
Trinity Hall, its magnificent extension now demolished, dominates the centre ground.

included in the demolition deal. Part of an address by the deputy managing
director of the development company to Aberdeen Chamber of Commerce is
worth quoting:

> Architecturally they had little unity of relationship with the adjoin-
> ing Music Hall building, but even so, when my company purchased
> the interests of both the Royal Northern Club and the YMCA we
> insisted that careful consideration be given to the design of the
> proposed development. The new development will form a more
> effective architectural composition both in relationship to the
> adjoining buildings and Union Street as a whole than did the previ-
> ous buildings.

The reaction of members is not recorded.

The destruction of these buildings in 1963 was greeted with disbelief, angrily but fruitlessly opposed and still regretted by those who remember them. Their tatty replacement was described by the historian and journalist, Dr Alexander Keith, as 'a cross between an upright garden frame and a broiler house'.

Demolition was also taking place on the south side of Union Street at the block Nos 145–9 with Birrell, a sweet shop, and Godsons, a dress shop, on the ground floor and various offices as well as a temperance hotel above. This was an original building that had become run down, its interior much altered over the years. Though an integral part of the street, it was not thought worth keeping. The Littlewoods Organisation moved into a new building on the site in 1964. Primark, clearly resolved to offend no one, took over in 2007 with an exceptionally dull frontage.

MARKET STREET

The demolition of the New Market followed in 1971. Its loss in the face of widespread protest caused great anger and sadness in Aberdeen. Its creation was part of a major town planning scheme and should first be put in context.

Market Street as originally planned by Archibald Simpson, with walk-through arcades at the junction with Union Street. His new Post Office building is left, next to the arcade. Its opposite number, right is the entrance to the New Market.

Market Street was developed by Archibald Simpson in association with John
Smith during 1840–2, to open a prestigious route between the east end of
Union Street and the harbour. The plan was to break the new road through
'betwixt the Royal Hotel and the property of Mr John Hay'. It would be
developed 'along with the erection of public markets', (i.e. the New Market,
from which it took its name) and be 'in line with the Great North Road' – St
Nicholas Street and George Street. Much dilapidated property was removed
for its creation, including the 'wretched, huddled hovels of Putachieside',
which skirted the western slope of St Catherine's Hill. At its south end,
Market Street swept through a part of the Shiprow.

The buildings at the head of Market Street, on both sides of the road,
were carried out to the edge of the pavement by these formidable yet handsome arcades, which gave covered access to Union Street. The long-established Royal Hotel, a coaching inn, next door to the easterly arcade was
patronised by High Court judges on circuit. It was no Lemon Tree. Lord
Cockburn described the 'Royal' as 'stinking'. The judges were later pleased to
move down Market Street to Mr Douglas of Airyhall's new hotel.

Around 1900, John Falconer acquired the Royal Hotel for his expanding
drapery and fancy goods business and commemorated the old name of the

Market Street in its glory. The Douglas Hotel, right, is at the Shiprow corner.
It is now a 'Jarvis' with a modernised frontage.

*The dark building with the box on top was originally Simpson's Post Office of 1842,
with Peter Mitchell's little tobacco shop, left, prior to demolition.*

hotel by calling the store Falconer's 'Royal Buildings'. He expanded his business simply and effectively by acquiring his neighbours. The arcade next to
Falconers was removed around 1870, when the house of which it was a part,
No. 67 Union Street and No. 1 Market Street, was transformed into a branch
of the National Bank of Scotland. Next door to the bank was the long-established little tobacconist of Peter Mitchell at No. 3 Market Street, its door and
windows gamely echoing the arcaded theme of its larger neighbours. To the
south was the three-storey No. 5–9 Market Street designed by Archibald
Simpson in 1842 as Aberdeen's Post Office, to cope with demand after the
introduction of the penny postage two years earlier. It was built as a matching piece for the New Market entrance opposite, with an arcaded frontage
and giant order of antae (square pilasters or columns at each end of the building). It had an auspicious start, but as the importance of the street was lost
sight of, a disappointing existence and a sad end. In 1875 it was superseded
by a larger and more splendid Post Office at the foot of Market Street. The
redundant Simpson building was mistreated thereafter, the arcaded ground
floor cut into for shops and a photographic studio for G & W Morgan built
on the roof.

After Falconers was acquired by the House of Fraser, the name was
changed to Frasers. In 1983 plans to extend and refurbish it as 'one of the

finest departmental stores in Europe' were announced. The bank next door was acquired, its listed façade retained after some prodding from heritage societies, incorporated and redeveloped as part of the store. Mitchell's little tobacconist's shop, by then Frasers' 'Tobacco Pouch', and Simpson's listed Nos 5–9, were demolished and the space where they stood developed as a new part of the store. Frasers closed its doors at the end of 2002, and new tenants – three chain stores – have effectively destroyed the arcade-echoing façade which Frasers took some pains to create.

Market Street's westerly arcade formed the east gable of Style & Mantle, Costumiers and Furriers at No. 73 Union Street. All went by the late 1920s, making way for an art deco building with industrial overtones by George Watt for Montague Burton.

THE NEW MARKET

*

Archibald Simpson's New Market was a trendsetting covered mall with a cathedral-like interior, later copied all over Britain. Its creation was integral to the laying out of Market Street and Simpson's use of changing levels between Union Street, the new Hadden Street and the Green was hailed as a brilliant technical achievement. The main entrance was in Market Street, a high, wide, handsome and formidable granite façade. It was this entrance that stopped Sir John Betjeman in his tracks shortly after he arrived in Aberdeen in 1947 and was staying across at the Douglas Hotel. 'So bold, so simple in design, so colossal in proportion,' he said, 'I had seen nothing like it before or since.'

The New Market's original interior was a round-ended hall of some 320 feet on the ground floor, with butchers and poulterers occupying the arcaded shops lining the walls. Books and clothes were sold in the first-floor arcades and fish in the basement, where there was an exit to the Green. The opening in April 1842 was a glittering affair, with the length of the Great Hall traversed by five tables, 'laden with a profusion of wine and cake'. Two bands, three pipers of the 42nd Regiment and the scholars of Robert Gordon's Hospital supplied the musical entertainment.

The New Market was also popular with market gardeners selling neaps and kale and Scots codlins, jeely apples and rennets. Farmers' wives sold butter, cheese and eggs on long trestle tables at the east end of the main hall. There were refreshment rooms, organ grinders and 'loons with pouches filled wi' tatties' which they let fly at the familiar, often pathetic characters, the likes

The Market Street entrance to the New Market, which so impressed Betjeman.
Here it is dressed overall for the visit of Edward VII and Queen Alexandra in
1906 to inaugurate the Marischal College extension.

of 'Sawdust' Calder and 'Feel Roddie' Stewart who did odd jobs and hung around the place. The south side was more popular than the north and 'one foul dirty toilet was used by all the men and boys about the market'. In April 1882 the building burnt down, the blaze starting at a basket maker's stall. In just an hour only the walls were left intact. Several stallholders had jumped from windows; one man dying in the attempt. It was quickly rebuilt.

In modern times the Union Street entrance was more popular than the Market Street one, for all its grandeur. It was a long, narrow, echoing corridor, part of which stretched over the East Green by covered walkway. At the end, before the steps into the main hall, was an automaton, ancient and intriguing and always with a child with face pressed against the glass watching the fireman on his ladder rescuing the damsel in distress. My mother declined to put a penny in the slot to activate the tableau as she disapproved of other people getting the chance to watch for nothing. However over the years I managed to snatch a few glances.

The original New Market interior. Its lunette windows made it look like a railway station, and for a time in the 1840s it was proposed as such but nothing came of it.

The New Market on fire in 1882, showing the view from Hadden Street.

Overleaf. The New Market was quickly rebuilt, the interior looking grander than before though the structure of the roof was different.

The New Market as many Aberdonians would remember it.

In time most of the open stalls were replaced by homely shops and for those of us who as children scuffed our shoes in the New Market's sawdust, it is this later interior that remains in the consciousness; though on reflection the fruit and vegetable stalls on the north side, their tatties and leeks still bearing the rich soil of Aberdeenshire, may well have dated from the 1882 rebuild. All the well-known butchers had shops there, Williamson, Spence Alsop, John Laidlaw, Alex Lawrence, James Sangster and James McIntosh, vying with displays of sides of beef, poultry and game in and out of plumage, sausages, tripe, liver, pigs' trotters, sheeps' heads, cartons of jellied chicken, potted heid. One shop had a team of butchers perpetually skinning rabbits, which they did with merry quips and great expertise. There was a unique and indefinable smell, boosted at strategic points by odours from the noisy and cheerful People's Café, by boiling beetroot and market candy. The Ellon Stall sold butter, oatcakes, eggs, honey, poultry and home-made crowdie. There was Park the jeweller, Annie Fraser's toy and souvenir shop and Sweetie Thomson. In the slightly spooky gallery were Low's bookstall, a fortune teller, an engraver, and buttons and knitting wool from Maxwells, who later moved to George Street. Down the steep granite stairs near the fountain was the cool basement and its marble slabs, the realm of the fish stalls; Mrs Nicoll, William Anderson, Robert Garrow, J & A Leiper and E. W. Forbes, some of them Royal warrant holders.

The Princess Café next door at No. 101 Union Street, a posher part of the A. A. Laing catering empire than the People's Café, was the place for coffee and a rowie. The main restaurant was downstairs and at busy times, Mr Laing himself stood on the half-landing, directing the traffic. There were huge, murky oil paintings of the stag-at-bay genre and a favourite table beside a bay window that looked out over the Green – all gone. Today I can't even find where the entrance was.

The end of the New Market was a slow and painful business starting in 1958 with a failed takeover bid. As the 1960s went by speculation as to its fate was rife. In November 1968 Aberdeen's Labour town council discussed a proposal to demolish it to make way for redevelopment. Councillor John Smith, a future Labour lord provost and life peer, introduced an amendment that the existing Market Street frontage be retained. He felt that the council should not accept plans which would destroy 'one of the best-known and gracious granite exteriors in the city'. On the other hand, a well-known Tory baillie deplored the setting up of the city as 'a vast museum', critical that 'every objection should be made when people were willing to spend £2,000,000 or £3,000,000 in Aberdeen'. Opinions were not exactly split along party lines! But the counsels of Mammon prevailed. The new development would bring in three times as much in rates.

An inquiry into plans for the proposed redevelopment by Commercial Union Properties Ltd followed in June 1969 before a Parliamentary Commission. In spite of the arguments of two private objectors, Councillor Smith and the architect Leo Durnin, and a report from David Walker of the Scottish Development Department, stating that almost every architectural critic of recent times considered the site to be one of the greatest examples of architectural design, the Parliamentary Commission, after a three-day inquiry, approved the redevelopment. The New Market became blighted, a ghost of its former self in 1970 as traders moved out. It closed on 6 January 1971 and thereafter was speedily demolished in the face of widespread protest. In 1972 Dr Alexander Keith wrote of how the New Market 'which had survived the fire of 1882 has recently succumbed to the vandalism of Big Business as licensed by the Town Council'. The replacement shopping centre was greatly inferior in every way.

BACK TO UNION STREET

*

The roller coaster of demolitions and near-demolitions went on apace in Union Street in the 1970s. Was there any part of the granite heritage that was not under threat? Nos 20–4 was an attractive block in dressed granite with a dome and a rounded return to Broad Street, running as far north as the Netherkirkgate. It was owned by Esslemont & Mackintosh who, to cut a long story short, exchanged it in a deal with the city council for Nos 32–8, now E&M's Men's and Gifts department. Nos 20–4 was occupied by the city's gas showrooms, publicity office and the Singer Sewing Machine Shop for a time, but the council's ultimate plan to demolish the whole corner block to widen the entrance to Broad Street came to pass in 1970. (We have already noted its demise in relation to Broad Street.)

The dazzling new Trinity Hall building of the Seven Incorporated Trades at Union Bridge had so impressed Prince Albert in 1848 that its joint architect William Smith was appointed architect of the new Balmoral. (His father John died in 1852, before the new castle was begun.) The Trades moved again in the mid-1960s, to Great Western Road, and Littlewoods who were next door acquired the building. Its ground floor is best remembered for the popular Mcmillan's, there from around 1900, purveyors of gifts, china, prams and sports goods. Mcmillan's closed down in 1965 and the building stood sad and grimy for over ten years. The Secretary of State gave Littlewoods permission to demolish the B-listed Trinity Hall and it is greatly to their credit that the firm did not do so, but took pains to restore its most outstanding features, including the Great Hall and its hammer-beam ceiling, carrying them on a completely new structure. It reopened in November 1980 and is now the Trinity self-service restaurant.

In 1972 moves to demolish the handsome Royal Workshops for the Blind in Huntly Street, off Union Street, one of John Smith's principal surviving works, were averted, thanks not least to intervention by the new heritage societies who began to play a major role in the fight against civic vandalism. The Blind Asylum was successfully restored as Princewall House. Archibald Simpson's superb Royal Athenaeum, burnt down in 1973, was in danger of demolition but ultimately restored. Unfortunately its famous restaurant, Jimmy Hay's, was transformed into offices during the redevelopment. In 1973 the council planned to sweep away the Music Hall, but after a public enquiry,

*Right. Nos 20–4 Union Street, dressed overall in 1906,
demolished in 1970.*

Prior to demolition, the Clydesdale Bank, right, and the Majestic Cinema.
Amicable House, next but one, is still extant.

the scheme was rejected by the Secretary of State. The council decided to have a change of heart and by 1986 had it handsomely restored.

The Majestic Cinema closed in 1974 and was demolished along with its small but perfectly formed neighbour, the Clydesdale Bank of 1911. They were succeeded by a large modern office block which unfortunately came with a gloomy, outsize canopy, a curious green-greyish roof and a grid system of numerous small windows providing a hint of penal servitude.

The Capitol Cinema, dating from 1933, was closed in 1998, sold in 2002 and is now two nightclubs, its once-delightful art deco frontage sadly demeaned. The local shops are long gone. Andrew Collie, high-class grocer, and Italian warehousemen went in 1971. The closure of the elegant department store Watt & Grant in 1981 was much regretted. Instead of window shopping for the latest fashions, one can now watch folk eating chips out of a poke.

CHAPTER 7

ST NICHOLAS STREET
AND GEORGE STREET

INTRODUCTION – TANNERY STREET

*

New projects were in the air in Aberdeen when the distractions of the Jacobite Rising of 1745 were over. Much of the old loch west of the Gallowgate, whence Loch Street took its name, was reclaimed. In 1754 the Town Council purchased land from a Mrs Urquhart which enabled them to open a new street from the Schoolhill/Upperkirkgate junction to the future Loch Street, providing access to the residential area that was developing there. The Tannery Company was granted a feu on the east side of this new street which the council 'ordanit to be callit Tannerie' in the no-nonsense style that prevailed. Around 1790, George Street, named in honour of George III, was laid out north from Tannery Street by James Staats Forbes, the Queen Street merchant, and his colleagues. It was to be the alternative homestretch of the Inverurie turnpike, a 'direct, level and elegant access to the town', a residential and commercially attractive alternative to the tortuous, hilly and slum-ridden existing route via Mounthooly and the Gallowgate. This 'elegant access' appears in John Smith's Plan of 1808 as George's Street, and that's how older Aberdonians still refer to it.

ST NICHOLAS STREET

The important new thoroughfare of Union Street was completed in 1805. Linking Tannery Street with Union Street became a priority. Fortunately the distance between them was only about 300 yards so another new street, St Nicholas Street, was laid out to join the two, though it sliced through the west end of the Netherkirkgate. Tannery Street was widened and absorbed by George Street.

St Nicholas Street and the old Tannery section of George Street were not

189

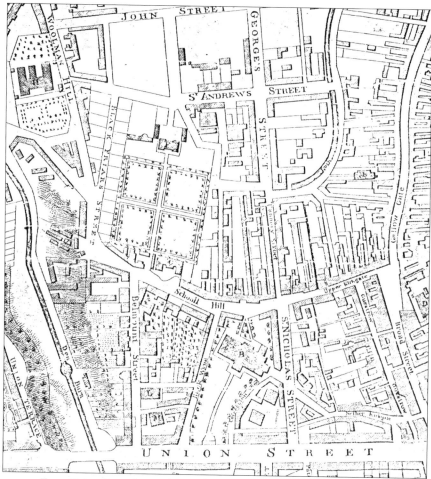

*From Union Street (bottom) St Nicholas Street (centre) heads north to the
Schoolhill/Upperkirkgate junction. Narrow Tannery Street continues northward to the
next junction at Loch Street, right, whose curves reflect its route along the bank of the
now-vanished loch. George's Street continues this new road northwards. Detail from
John Smith's Plan of 1808.*

subject to the architectural constraints that inhibited development in Union
Street, and were more easily accessible for most Aberdonians. In the first
quarter of the nineteenth century the modest confines of St Nicholas Street
boasted robust tenements of houses with shops on the ground floor thronged
with an array of merchants, manufacturers, advocates, seedsmen, ironmongers, tea dealers, engravers, dressmakers, milliners, bakers, druggists, shoe-
makers, watchmakers, wigmakers, fishing tackle and gunmakers, a cork

manufacturer, a stoneware merchant, a surgeon, an artist, a hosier and a pattern-making establishment. The well-known jewellers A & J Smith, and Martin the Butcher, were early on the scene. Above all, St Nicholas Street became renowned for its tailors and drapers and the vibrancy of its advertising. 'Why go west?' (i.e. to Union Street) was a favorite theme. St Nicholas Street quickly became Aberdeen's most popular shopping area, and remained so until the end.

'THE QUEEN'
*

In 1866 a fine marble statue of the young Queen Victoria by the Footdee sculptor Alexander Brodie was erected at the junction of Union Street and St Nicholas Street, on the east side. In 1888, with the marble deteriorating, she

One of the best-known views in Aberdeen. Just beyond 'The Queen' (on the right), Reith Bros proclaim their wares on the gable-end of No. 2, a popular advertising site for several St Nicholas Street drapers. Left, No. 72 Union Street, its elegance jazzed up by H. Samuel, turns a graceful corner to become No. 1 St Nicholas Street. It formed the east end of the old Gloucester Hotel block and its demise was noted in Chapter 6.

was taken down and transported to the shelter of the Town House vestibule, to be replaced in 1893 by the statue of an older Queen in bronze by C.B. Birch. Along with the 'Monkey House' at the Union Street/Terrace junction, 'The Queen' was the Aberdonians' favourite meeting place for a century. She was removed to the Queen's Cross roundabout in 1964; not entirely lost, but certainly missed from her original stance.

THE EAST SIDE

'THE QUEEN' TO THE NETHERKIRKGATE

*

Going along to the east side of St Nicholas Street, Reith Bros and their successors, Claude Alexander, operated from 'Queen's Corner', No. 2. Next to them was a baker, latterly Strathdee, with the famous Rubber Shop at the

The London Rubber Co. at No. 16 St Nicholas Street before it became the Rubber Shop. It took over No. 18 on the Netherkirkgate corner as well. It was owned by the Fowler family throughout its existence.

Right. The west end of the Netherkirkgate in the 1920s, with the Wallace Tower as pub. A dim 'Toys' sign indicates the Rubber Shop, and Fyffe the Brushmaker would have been opposite. This area had vanished by 1964. The junction with St Nicholas Street is beyond, with the edge of the handsome Montague Burton building in view. The East Kirk of St Nicholas towers above.

The west end of the Netherkirkgate, the same area as shown on page 193, but the view, looking east from East St Nicholas Kirk, is reversed. Marks & Spencers, left, has replaced Raggy Morrisons and Jeans Fashions, the Rubber Shop. The 'closing down sale' signs indicate 1963 when the area was demolished to make way for a new M&S. The Wallace Tower, its days numbered, peeps coyly out between 'Jeans' and the Frigate bar.

Netherkirkgate corner stretching back as far as the Wallace Tower. In the early years of the twentieth century, as the London Rubber Co., it was advertising 'really good' waterproof garments, footballs, rubber shoes, hosepipes, rubber collars and cycle inner tubes and, by the 1920s, camping equipment to cater for the outdoors' boom after the First World War. Those who were children during the '40s and '50s remember an artificial bird in a cage which would sing if you put a penny in the slot, and an early Santa's grotto down rickety stairs in the basement. The Rubber Shop flitted to Nos 12–16 George Street at the end of the last war and Jean's Fashion Shop moved in.

On the other side of the Netherkirkgate junction was the old established business of John Fyffe, Brushmaker to Her Majesty. From 1835 for over half a century his premises were at No. 22 St Nicholas Street opposite the Rubber Shop. Then Fyffe moved further into the Netherkirkgate, combining shop and workshop, all handsomely rebuilt, steam-powered and proudly displaying the

Royal Warrant. The funds to modernise came from a deal with William Morrison, draper, who had already acquired No. 20 in 1886 after the fire at Black's Buildings. Morrison now expanded into No. 22. 'Raggy' Morrison's, as the shop was invariably called, was sparsely fitted out and had rough wooden floors, but it was Aberdeen's most popular cut-price store, selling everything from books to brushes, china to carpets, sometimes hanging eye-catching items, even a piano, from the ceiling. Raggy's specialised in dress-making material and remnants, often from bankrupt stock. Morrison went into partnership with James Mearns, initially a poor loon from Kintore who prospered so much as a director of Raggy's that he leased Aboyne Castle from the Marquis of Huntly. Mearns died in 1943 and the following year, Nos 20–2 was acquired by Marks & Spencer.

THE NETHERKIRKGATE TO FLOURMILL BRAE
*

If Raggy's was the most famous drapery in St Nicholas Street, it was by no means the only one. Baillie James Kinghorn at Nos 30–4 at the other end of the spectrum, offered the smartest dress-making establishment in Aberdeen, with fitting rooms and waiting rooms, as well as an emporium with French

Left. The Equitable in the foreground, Smarts, centre, and 'Raggy' Morrisons, later M&S, right.

Right. A pristine Equitable building, complete with awnings and pedimented windows on the first floor.

and English millinery, fur coats, stoles and bed and table linen After the last war, Smarts, the furnishing chain took over the premises. Next door, on the corner with Flourmill Brae was another Aberdeen favourite, the 'Equitable'. The accent was on the second syllable. Like Raggy's, it was a sale shop where everything was reduced. It was a sparse place too, but with a considerable and continually changing range of goods.

FLOURMILL BRAE
TO THE UPPERKIRKGATE
*

The 'Woolies' block was handsome but austere with emphasis on string courses and granite blocks of varied shades. In the nineteenth century the office of the city police commissioners was based here. McIntosh & Mackie, drapers and furriers, occupied No. 46 on the Flourmill corner, described in the *Bon Accord* of 1907 as 'old-established'. 'The Electric Lift will convey you to Fur Coats, Fur-Trimmed Coats, Raincoats on Second Floor' one of their advertisements ran. By the early 1950s Vogue Fashions had taken over.

Next door at Nos 50–2 and making its appearance around 1919 with its soon-to-be familiar fascia of chunky gilt lettering against red was F. W.

Left. The 'Woolies' block with 'Vogue' fashions on the corner and Woolworths centre.

Right. The 'Woolies' block from Flourmill Lane showing the side entrance, left. This is a building that would have responded to restoration.

Woolworth & Co, 'little Woolies' or 'George Street Woolies' as it was frequently, if inaccurately, called. The toiletries counter specialised in large jars of edible-looking frosty bath crystals and 'Californian Poppy' perfume, which smelt nice. It was sometime before I learned of its notoriety. A tagged-on hardware department at the back sold paint, shoelaces, tennis balls and deckchairs, and, as at the Rubber Shop, you could feel the difference in floor levels. A side door gave access to Flourmill Brae, allowing you to cut across to enter the Equitable by another side door, or vice versa.

At No. 56 Taylor's Mantle Shop supplied not gowns but gas mantles for many years and George Bowman's Mourning Warehouse was at Nos 58–60. It was well known in its day when mourning dress and widows' weeds were *de rigueur.* Bowman's carried a large stock, but could, if required, quickly make up veiling, umbrellas, mantles of the other sort and, somewhat strangely, corsets for the bereaved. By 1925 Alex Scott & Co, tailor and outfitters were trading at these premises. As well as stocking ready-to-wear clothes, Scott's tailoring department made morning coats in black vicuna, evening wear in black barathea. It specialised in kitting out uniform wearers, from the Armed Forces to the Brownies. Next door at No. 62 was the well-known ironmonger Michie Watt, while the last shop before the Upperkirkgate was Boots the Chemist at No. 68 with its distinctive hipped roof. It was managed for many years by Charlie McKay, a chamber music enthusiast.

THE WEST SIDE

CORRECTION WYND TO SCHOOLHILL

*

At the start of this block, at Nos 29–31, was the long-established jeweller, Louis Reis, a calm, unhurried place near one of the entrances to St Nicholas Kirk, with a hypnotic wag-at-the-wa' clock and a pleasant smell of polish. Cable Shoes, later Curtess, was next door. Ugly fascias had come into vogue when the photo overleaf was taken *c.* 1980. Just beyond Curtess and at an earlier date was a linen warehouse (the old name for a large shop) at No. 39–43, belonging to Peter Beveridge, who sold 'real Aberdeen wincey'. The other shops are not so easy to make out in the photo but they included Parkinson the ladies outfitter at Nos 45–7, a fixture for many years. An earlier occupant was George Souter, a high-class tailor, hatter and Boys' Brigade officer who supplied Boys' Brigade uniforms. Alex Booth, a quality hatter,

This block began with Louis Reis the jeweller and ended with Reid & Pearson.

was next door at Nos 49–51, with the Aberdeen Clothing Company, owned by Robert Grate, who traded in overalls, boiler suits and dungarees, at Nos 53–5. Both shops were taken over by Jackson the Tailors. Tucked out of sight are Stevenson & Russell and Jerome's, the popular photographers who sold post-card-sized photos at three for 1/6 during the war (Kirkcaldy Linoleum moved in later). Finally, there was Reid & Pearson's. The turreted building on the extreme right, No. 1 George Street, James Rust, 1891, architect, marks the Schoolhill-George Street junction.

Reid & Pearson's was a household name but neither Andrew B. Reid nor John Pearson lived to see their fine new shop at the end of St Nicholas Street. Reid and Pearson, both experienced in the trade, opened a new drapery store at No. 19 George Street in 1905 with a staff of three. John Pearson, the benefactor behind the Pearson Picnics so beloved of the Upper Fittie bairns, continued solo after Reid's retirement a few years later. Pearson died in 1914 not long after opening a Union Street branch and the business was taken over by Mrs Potts, Reid & Pearson's first employee, and her husband, Sydney. The Potts took the bold step of closing down both shops, acquiring Nos 61–5 St Nicholas Street and opening a striking new store quite unlike anything else in the city, on the corner of Schoolhill in 1926. Demolition in Schoolhill was necessary to allow the display windows to continue round from St Nicholas Street as far as the graveyard. The windows,

Reid & Pearson in the 1950s, with the ballroom on the top floor. No other shop looked quite like it. Jerome's (or Kirkcaldy Linoleum) was next door, and then at No 55a, the church gateway shop of Stevenson & Russell discussed overleaf.

with their heavy brass surrounds, were cleaned every morning by a team of disabled men.

Like all St Nicholas Street drapers, Reid & Pearson had its specialities; artificial flowers for trimming hats; tartan skirts; and sheepskin jackets. On their retirement in 1949, the Potts sold the business to the Scottish Drapery Corporation. This was taken over three years later by Hugh Fraser, who retained the original name, as he did with Watt & Grant. John Robbie was manager until the end in May 1973. Until it was demolished, the shop's fine display windows advertised local events.

In the post-war area there were grumbles about the amount of traffic in a confined area, but it was only at certain times that St Nicholas Street was particularly busy, and that was part of its charm. Trams were singled-out as causing a 'bottleneck' at the south end of St Nicholas Street and abolished from that route.

THE END OF THE WALLACE TOWER
*

Buses were introduced in 1955. They did not have the same charisma as trams and created even bigger traffic problems, some argued. Meanwhile Boots the Chemist at No. 68 was pulled down as part of the scheme to widen

*Stevenson & Russell, watchmakers and opticians, occupied St Nicholas Street's
most unusual shop at No. 55a. Dating from 1822, it was the original entry to St
Nicholas kirkyard from St Nicholas Street. It had a classical frontage in Rubislaw
granite, flanked by pilasters with a pediment above containing an attic (housing the
gatekeeper). It was converted into a very small shop before the end of the nineteenth
century, with the stonework of the old gateway retained as the frontage. Mr Russell
looked after the town's clocks as well as those at Balmoral, and the frontage
had room proudly to display the Royal Warrant as well as the optician's
pince-nez sign. By J.A. Sutherland.*

*Right. The trams of St Nicholas Street, a scene that has passed into history. In 1964
this whole street was designated Area A, of the CCDA, 1.59 acres, destined for total
destruction, as was Area B beyond which totalled almost 10 acres.*

the south side of the Upperkirkgate. The St Nicholas Street-Netherkirkgate
junction was also denounced as a major contributor to this bottleneck and in
the early 1960s a solution was devised by Marks & Spencer, still in the old
'Raggy' Morrison building, and Aberdeen Town Council, which would kill
two birds with one stone. M&S contrived an improved site for themselves,

nearer Union Street, by building a new store adjacent to their old one, lying across the west end of the Netherkirkgate and clearing the bottleneck by obliterating it. Unfortunately this scheme not only involved the destruction of part of the Netherkirkgate, but it was also apparently 'necessary for the Wallace Tower (Benholm's Lodging) to be demolished in consequence of proposals for the widening and redevelopment of the Netherkirkgate'. By the end of 1962 opposition to the demolition of the 'B'-listed Tower was growing and both the Scottish Development Department and the Ancient Monuments Board, according to an Aberdeen Town Council Minute of 19 April 1963:

> Made strong representations about the importance of preserving the said building on the grounds of architectural merit and historic interest, but had been unable to suggest how the building might be retained on its present site consistently with the carrying out of the proposed redevelopment.

Given that there was alternative access, a more satisfactory approach would have been to designate the relevant part of the Netherkirkgate a pedestrian precinct and to suggest that Marks & Spencer look elsewhere for more suitable premises. (It was too late by 1963, but the old Palace Hotel site, cleared in 1950, would have been appropriate.) For good measure it could have been suggested that the Wallace Tower be given the major restoration it deserved, courtyard and garden reinstated and at the same time Carnegie's Brae made an attractive approach to the Green and not the apparent descent into hell that it has been as long as I can remember. Instead the council was delighted and the Ancient Monumentalists, one suspects, were relieved when M&S offered to meet the cost of demolishing the Wallace Tower and re-erecting it elsewhere.

Edward Meldrum summed up in *Aberdeen of Old:*

> Benholm's Lodging was demolished with part of the Netherkirkgate despite the strongest protests, to make way for a store. A large undistinguished structure replaced a unique example of a Z-plan townhouse within a Scots town ... Although a replica building, incorporating some of the stonework and features of the demolished townhouse was erected in 1964 in Tillydrone Road, both the demolition and the pseudo-towerhouse showed a serious lack of understanding by the Scottish Office and the city council of the real meaning and purpose of conservation of our historic buildings and their environment.

This lamentable episode is commemorated by a sycophantic and erroneous plaque which fortunately languishes in obscurity in Carnegie's Brae.

By the 1960s, as already touched on in the Upperkirkgate section, the city council was convinced that this popular shopping area, St Nicholas Street (Area A) and George Street as far as Loch Street, bounded by Harriet Street on the west and the Gallowgate on the east (Area B) required to be completely demolished and rebuilt. The St Nicholas area of over an acre and half was to be tackled first. In the intervening years before redevelopment St Nicholas Street became a half-hearted pedestrian precinct with buses, bicycles, service vehicles and various permit holders curtailing the freedom of anyone rash enough to walk on the road. In autumn 1982 Aberdeen City Council in a multi-million redevelopment in partnership with Great Universal Stores, began the demolition of St Nicholas Street, which was replaced by a closed mall of continuous chain stores with a largely unfrequented upper deck. Retailers moved out with regret. The development seems to have taken many people by surprise, for the old familiar shops did not seem particularly run down. They were genuinely missed and the St Nicholas scheme was roundly condemned by the Royal Fine Art Society for its treatment of the townscape.

GEORGE STREET

We can move on now to George Street. The section from the Upperkirkgate – Schoolhill junction to Loch Street was the old Tannery Street. This of course was the backbone of Area B of the 10-acre redevelopment scheme. Ironically, the original George Street, which started at Loch Street, was outside the scheme.

THE EAST SIDE

UPPERKIRKGATE TO LOCH STREET
*

For over fifty years, Nos 2–8 George Street, Tyler's shoe shop, was located at the start of the east side. The whole of this listed block, including the lower part of the Upperkirkgate, survives as Burger King. There was a Buttermilk Dairy next door at No. 10a, which in the 1950s became a Barnett's Orange

Ghost town. George Street between the Upperkirkgate and Loch Street waiting to be knocked down in 1987. Demolition started with the block on the right that had the Rubber Shop at the centre. Here the stonework had delicate enrichment and, with more sympathetic frontages, would have made a stylish block. In the distance across the Loch Street divide is the infamous skulking ziggurat of Norco House, as it then was. Extreme left is the lower half of the turreted No. 1 George Street. The fine details are apparent. After being a men-only bar it became a Next fashion shop. It survives along with the former Tylers opposite, both now flanking the entrance to the Bon Accord Centre, the shops and parking complex. Unfortunately a huge glass canopy, burger-eaters and hanging baskets distract the eye from these elegant buildings .

Grove, so small that there was always a queue outside. Then there was the Rubber Shop, transplanted from St Nicholas Street, which had a little arcade and a good selection of sports goods on the lower floor. More familiar names followed; Argo, outfitters; Meldrums, an excellent and popular tailor; Timpson the shoeshop; and Menzies & Sons, outfitters, at Nos 44–8 from 1935 till the end, their art deco frontage designed by George Bennet Mitchell & Son.

At Nos 52–8 the United Presbyterian (U.P.) Church of 1821 devised a building that could easily be converted into a warehouse in case they were not successful. Understated embellishment was visible on the façade until the end. (In the event they were so successful that one of their elders, the architect R.G. Wilson, designed the cathedral-like Carden Place U.P. church for them, later Melville-Carden Place Church which is now handsomely converted into offices.) Reid & Bain acquired the premises and sold marmot, fitch, grebe, white hare, tibet skunk, opossum, stone marten and more. An exotic pet shop? No, a fur shop. After the war, the wallpaper shops, Morris Wallpaper at No. 56 and the West Riding Wallpaper Company at No. 62, were always crowded out whenever one passed. G. S. Cowie, a gent's outfitters, both popular and superior, was near the junction with Loch Street. Finally, on the corner was the little A. B. Hutchison snackbar, The Buttery.

LOCH STREET

THE CO-OP ARCADE

*

On reaching The Buttery, the feet used to automatically turn into Loch Street, past the Loch Street branch Post Office with its little brass rail and the Swan Bar, then the junction with the north end of Drum's Lane.

Carrying on round, were St Paul Street School, a teachers' resource centre and musical instruments repository at the end of its days and St Paul's Episcopal Church with its handsome spire. Its predecessor, Old St Paul's Chapel, was normally entered from the Gallowgate, but had a rear entrance from the Lochside (later Loch Street) where a circular patch of grass surrounded by a cobbled drive was laid out for the convenience of those who came to worship by carriage. The 'new' church of 1865 faced out to Loch Street and the grassy patch and carriage drive became the front approach. Next to the church were the headquarters of the Northern Co-operative Society and its famous arcade building.

The trim Loch Street Post Office and the Swan Bar.

The popular Buttery on the George Street/Loch Street corner bites the dust.
The Loch Street Post Office is covered in scaffolding and the fascia of the
Swan Bar peeps over the hoarding.

Drum's Lane at its junction with Loch Street, by I. W. Davidson.
The old Soup Kitchen lies beyond.

The Loch Street triumvirate. From right, St Paul Street School, 1873, St Paul's
Episcopal Church, 1865, and the Northern Co-operative building, the second on
the site, 1905. All three were demolished in 1986.

The original Northern Co-op HQ in 1883, William Henderson architect, strong and
simple with effective fenestration, arcading, corbie steps at the gable-end and a touch of
the agricultural – reminiscent of stabling at the fairmtoon of a wealthy farmer, perhaps?
It makes an interesting comparison with the building of 1906, (p.216)

That great Aberdeen institution, the Northern Co-operative (originally
Company) Society Ltd, was founded in 1861. The directors ran a tight ship,
making every penny count, and in 1873 were able to purchase a large piece of
ground lying between the Gallowgate and Loch Street for £2,305 to build
headquarters worthy of their now-flourishing enterprise. The building was
remodelled in 1906, in a simple yet robust style, recalling Henry Gray's new
emporium at the Upperkirkgate/Broad Street junction. It had string courses,
cartouches, pillars and pilasters and had grown upwards! The entrance has
an echo of St Paul's Gateway in the Gallowgate. From here stairs led up to
the Climax office where cheques were sorted out in preparation for the 'Divi',
a red-letter day in Aberdeen life. Of collecting the 'Divi' Arthur Bruce writes:

The famous arcade in primitive mode.
It was later repaved and roofed over with glass.

To a child it was an adventure. In the course of moving along in the seemingly never-ending queue, stairs were climbed, doors and passages passed through which were normally forbidden territory. Characters were encountered who were surely the inspiration for many of Harry Gordon's Comic Wifie roles.

The arcade, a covered shopping mall, had a distinctive, indefinable smell – of groceries, perhaps. The grocery department was near the entrance on the left-hand side, with two counters for different items, both always so busy that there was always a wait. The shoe department was at the far end of the arcade, its navy leather seats and footstools, shoehorns, foot-measuring rulers and mirrors still clearly remembered by many. The steps on the right-hand side led up to fashions, millinery and tearoom. This was a place of aerial delights, where money and the precious Co-op cheques flew between counter and cashdesk in little brass cylinders.

Staff from the Climax office at the east end of the arcade in the 1940s. The arch, left, was a pend containing stairs, not visible, which took one out to the Gallowgate. The handsome Roman temple, right, if fully seen would reveal itself as a beautiful fountain in pink granite, 'Erected in honour of the founders of the Northern Co-operative Company Limited 1861–1911'.

The last days of the Co-op Arcade. The shoe department had been on the left, fashions, millinery, tearoom etc on the higher level, right. The handsome fountain, top right, was taken to Norco's, later the Scottish Co-op's premises at Berryden, where it was prominently displayed. Surplus to requirements after Sainsbury's took over, it is in storage at a Westhill granite yard, awaiting relocation to the Scottish Co-op's Funeralcare in Rose Street, Aberdeen. Here it will go on show again.

LOCH STREET TO
ST ANDREW STREET
✳

Most of this section of George Street, from Nos 88–142, and the correspon-
ding section of Loch Street facing the Arcade, was owned by the Northern
Co-op. Here the Society had a number of shops and confectioners, including
a tobacconist, a chemist and a furniture shop, and after the First World War
it was planned to replace them with a grand entrance on the prominent thoroughfare of George Street, leading through to the Loch Street arcade. This
never happened, but there was something exciting for the young shopper
here, a short cut between George Street and Loch Street, through a narrow
close entered from an anonymous door between the shops, with much
opening and shutting of doors. The middle section was under the skies. Then
one emerged in Loch Street opposite the Co-op. If it was Christmas and the
decorations were up, it was a magical scene. The arcade had transformed
itself into a wonderland, with tiny fairy lights from Italy, a frieze of icicles
from Denmark and silver trees from Germany. Huge panels showing
Cinderella or Snow White were the work of a local artist, and all the frames,
animation and wiring were made in the Co-op's own workshops and engi-
neering department. The 'Co-opie Lights' were famous and drew crowds
from far and wide.

THE WEST SIDE

SCHOOLHILL TO
'LITTLE' LOCH STREET
✳

We can go back now to look at the west side, from the Schoolhill junction.
Beyond the turreted pub at No. 1 were many familiar names: Cooper's Stores,
the ubiquitous Claude Alexander and A & J Scott, clothiers at No. 29. (The
Scott brothers had fallen out and Alex, already encountered, had set up in St
Nicholas Street.) Then John Martin the butcher, at No. 31, Gordon's the
chemists at No. 35, the Scotch Wool Shop at Nos 43–4 and at Nos 51–3, Bruce
Miller, music sellers. 'Nothing was ever too much for the staff, from Mr
Wood the Human Gramophone Catalogue to Miss Downie and Miss Buyers
at the music counter,' recalls Arthur Bruce. Then there was The Hosiery,
which also had a Union Street shop, and Parkinson's Ladies' Outfitters, later
a Clydesdale radio and electrical shop, at the junction with 'little' Loch Street.

Left. The ghost town again. The west side of George Street between Schoolhill and Loch Street.
Right. The Hosiery, No. 83, and the Clydesdale, No. 85, with handsome curving chimney stack before demolition. A good scrub and discreet fascias would have worked wonders.

Close-up of the windows of one of the buildings, top left, ornamented with triangular and elliptical pediments.

Demolition in George Street viewed from Crooked Lane.

LOCH STREET
TO ST ANDREW STREET

ISAAC BENZIES

*

This part of George Street was opposite the Norco House ziggurat. The buildings have survived, though not the original shops. Particularly worthy of
mention was Isaac Benzie. Born at Oyne in 1865, the youngest of six, he
worked on the family farm, then entered the drapery trade and in 1894
started up on his own at No. 185 George Street, in premises later occupied by
J. & W. Cameron. This was a brave step given the presence of the Northern
Co-operative in nearby Loch Street with its siren song of the 'Divi' and cut-
throat competition from neighbouring drapers. But he was a skilled hosier
whose own make of stockings was famous locally, and a canny retailer. By
1919 he owned Nos 143–67, a fair skelp of George Street, and a truly remarkable department store arose out of this motley collection of properties which
had included a furniture shop, a butcher's, Ligertwood's Court at No. 147, a
shoemaker's, a tailor's, a pharmacist's and a number of tenements.

By 1924 all his business was concentrated under one roof, or rather
several adjoining roofs, and the creation of an arcade along the George Street
frontage and turrets at the St Andrew's Street corners gave a sense of unifor-

213

mity. Specialities included a dressmaking materials' hall on the ground floor, excellent china and crockery departments, the largest millinery department in Scotland, a baby carriage room, a hairdressers, a superior Ladies', a chiropodist and a smokeroom. In these days before tenement conversions were thought of, I.B.'s handsomely tiled private bathrooms, where soft, warm, fresh-smelling towels were available at a small extra charge, were much appreciated by the local clientele. The tearoom, with its famous string trio, has passed into Aberdeen legend.

Isaac Benzie died in 1926 after a life of hard work and the real achievement of creating in the east end of town a department store which had style and which was a favourite with all classes. He was succeeded by his sons, Isaac and (afterwards) Athol who was prominent in civic life. I.B.'s was sold to the House of Fraser in 1955. There was a major refurbishment and all the original polished mahogany and brass shopfittings thrown out. In 1972 the store was renamed Arnotts, but that name never caught on.

This advertisement shows how skilfully Isaac Benzies unified diverse frontages.

THE BEGINNING
OF THE END
*

Meanwhile, the Northern Co-operative Society, having given up the great frontage idea, demolished the Loch Street-St Andrew Street section of George Street and in 1970 opened a massive new store there, Norco House, with everything under one roof. Hailed as 'synonymous with all that is best in modern shopping' by a spokesperson, this massively tiered ziggurat was variously described as 'ugly', 'aggressive' and 'a horror', and that was just the Co-op directors. Though it was outside Area B of the CCDA, it was intended to stand square with this development, profiting from the number of people shopping at the new centre. Area B, however, was bogged down by public inquiries and Norco House, for all its convenience, never had the same appeal as the now-abandoned arcade. It had arrived too early on the scene. By 1986 the Northern Co-op was in difficulties, and the on-going upheaval in George Street and the opening of the St Nicholas Centre were blamed for the decreasing numbers of customers at Norco House. The Northern Co-op would go out of business in 1993. It was a sad day for a great institution, but it had seriously overreached itself by building a superstore at Berryden at the same time as Norco House*. The city council had meanwhile acquired the arcade in 1973 with a view to demolition and blight had set in. The building was demolished in 1986 and nothing was built where it stood.

The CCDA generated three major public inquiries. Over 40 per cent of the shops in the area were locally owned and at the first public inquiry in 1975, the George Street traders ran a well-planned campaign, illustrating how the traditional courts and closes could be regenerated, open spaces created, additional and improved housing provided and the many fine granite buildings in the area expertly restored. Even the Secretary of State suggested preservation, to no avail. In 1976 the whole scheme was almost voted out by councillors, but Labour dissenters were whipped-in, and five Tory mavericks

* Norco House was sold to Bredero in 1985, and on to John Lewis. An attempt was made to re-jig the building as an architecturally more ordinary store, a ziggurat caché as it were. The bakers A.B. Hutchison whose trade had been badly affected by the upheaval went out of business and their exuberant Central Bakery building at 123 George Street in Aberdeen Triumphant style (Brown & Watt, 1897) was sold to Bredero in 1986. Isaac Benzies (Arnotts) also closed down in 1986 because trading was so poor, after years of upheaval. Grand refurbishments in the French style were promised, but the whole building is, in a sense, lost. It is still there, on the fringe of the Bon Accord Centre but divided into shop units and flats, scarcely recognisable and almost forgotten.

voted with the Labour group. Eventually objectors were overruled and Aberdeen City Council formed a partnership with a Dutch firm, Bredero, to develop Area B. Work began in 1985 though there was unease that the local authority should be both joint developer and planning authority. In all the 'blighted' years, no discussions took place between the powers-that-be and property owners and retailers about ways of improving the area other than by wholesale demolition.

At the end of the day, all 10 acres of Area B came down and the Bon Accord Centre, surely a misnomer, went up, in spite of all the 'hype' and blandishment an ordinary 1960s-style centre filled with the sort of shops one sees everywhere else. The trauma had endured for nearly thirty years, until 1990 when the Queen opened the Centre, quietly expressing concern about the fate of Union Street.

Still standing proud, the Co-op headquarters of 1906 awaits demolition in 1986.

PART 3
Burgh of Barony

*

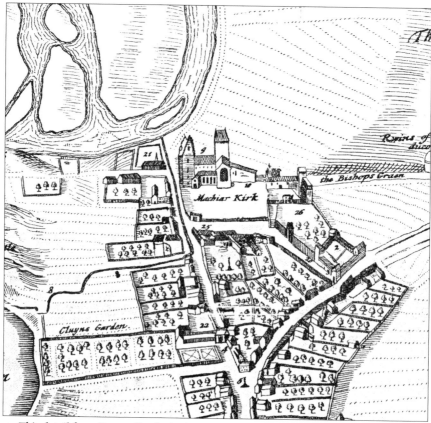

*This detail from Parson Gordon's Plan, 1661, shows the north end of Old Aberdeen.
Centre, the long avenue of the Chanonry, flanked by a few manses and their glebes.
Cluny's Garden is to the left, stretching to the Loch of Old Aberdeen. St Machar's
Cathedral is at the top with, from left, twin towers, nave with marriage porch, the tower
and its saddleback roof with the south transept in front, and finally a diminished choir
at the right end. Right again is the Bishop's Palace and its garden (26). The drawing of
the palace does not have Gordon's usual detail because at this very time, Dr William
Guild, then principal of King's College, was dismantling it, using the 'great joists and the
stately timber work' to hold his crumbling college together. Dunbar Hall of Residence
was later built on this site. It was demolished c. 2000 and the area awaits redevelopment. The quadrangle below, (2), is the Chaplains' Chambers, built by Gavin Dunbar in
1519 as a hall of residence for the chaplains of the cathedral. It was built round a square
courtyard with towers in the corner, and a well. The south-west ranges survive as
Chaplains' Court, a contender for the title of oldest house in Aberdeen. The Marquis of
Huntly's townhouse (25) is opposite the cathedral. His great garden lies behind, formed
by enclosing the glebes of Belhelvie, Daviot and Forbes manses. Left of St Machar's is
Gavin Dunbar's Hospital (21) with its little spire. The glebe of Monymusk manse, worked
by the beadsmen, is left again, but the manse has gone, its stones recycled.*

CHAPTER 8

OLD ABERDEEN

Old Aberdeen, arguably, is neither old nor is it Aberdeen. It lies almost two miles north of the Granite City at the mouth of the Don rather than the Dee (as 'Aberdeen' might imply) and it became a burgh of barony only in 1489 while Aberdeen, as indicated in a charter of King William the Lion, was confirmed as a Royal burgh as early as 1165. However, the origins of the Old Aberdeen are undeniably ancient. The delightful legend of its founding, of Machar sent by Columba in the sixth century to establish a church where a river curved like a shepherd's crook, may have invoked the scepticism of scholars; yet they cannot deny a Christian presence in that area around the seventh century, as revealed by a boulder, the Seaton Stone, a Class III Pictish stone incised with a cross. Old Aberdeen probably began life not as a village but as an ecclesiastical settlement, the shadowy Kirkton of Seaton in the vicinity of the present Seaton Park, perhaps a church of turf walls and a heather-thackit roof with a few simple dwellings nearby.

Centuries later, David I, who reigned from 1124–53, reorganised the structure of the native church and created a new diocese of Aberdeen which covered much of north-east Scotland. The headquarters were not, as one might expect, in the thriving burgh of Aberdeen, where the grand Mither Kirk of St Nicholas was already taking shape, but two miles to the north at the Kirkton, which the legendary presence of St Machar had endowed with a special sanctity. David I relocated the pious Culdee, Nectan, from Mortlach in Banffshire as its first bishop and provided generous endowments in lands and revenue.

THE CHANONRY

St Machar's Cathedral
*

St Machar's, you may argue, is not lost and this is true. It is only half lost, the result not so much of a 'dinging doon' by the reforming mobs of 1560 but of a fatal blend of the later activities of their co-religionists and various Acts of God.

As time went by St Machar's bishops evolved from holy men to great officers of state and their seat changed from a simple turf-and-heather chapel to a cathedral that reflected their status. In 1282 the new bishop Henry de Cheyne decided the existing St Machar's was 'not glorious enough' and began a new one in the same place, starting with the choir, the clergy's sanctum at the east end. Other bishops appeared on site from time to time with even more glorious sets of plans. However the attempts of even the keenest builder-bishops were too often frustrated by the intervention of royal business or death. At last, by the mid-sixteenth century completion was at hand. The great Bishop William Elphinstone (1483–1514), consolidated the great central tower in 1511 adding a lead-covered timber spire, then embarked on an extensive replacement for Henry de Cheyne's thirteenth-century choir. He had almost finished when he died of a broken heart following the disastrous defeat at the Battle of Flodden. Putting the finishing touches on the choir was not on the agenda of Elphinstone's successor, Bishop Gavin Dunbar (1518–32), though he created the famous heraldic ceiling, not so much an overview of contemporary Christendom as a coded sequence of brickbats and bouquets for some of its leading lights. He also dismantled Bishop Henry de Lictoun's confrontational caphouses, which had gone up as a defensive measure after the Battle of 'reid Harlaw' of 1411, replacing them with the cathedral's 'trademark' twin spires of Moray sandstone. Finally he had the south transept, 'Dunbar's Aisle', prepared as his burial ground.

The cathedral was almost finished when the Reformation burst on Aberdeen in 1560. The 'rascal multitude' had time to do no more than burn the library, before the intervention of the Earl of Huntly and his posse. As sheriff of Aberdeen, bailie of the diocese, head of the House of Gordon, leader of Scottish Catholics and the incumbent bishop's nephew, Huntly was just the person to see them off. Then the cathedral began to disappear. First, the loose stones of Elphinstone's incomplete choir at the east end, surplus to the needs of the reformed religion, were spirited away by Old Aberdeen's DIY enthusiasts. Next, in 1568, the privy council ordered that lead be stripped from St Machar's to pay the army of the Earl of Moray, campaigning in the north against the supporters of Mary, Queen of Scots. Weakened by the loss of lead, the spire fell a few years later in 'the violence of a great storme of winde'.

The occupation of Scotland in the 1650s by Cromwell's troops under General Monck was the indirect cause of St Machar's greatest disaster. To build their fort in the Castlehill, the English soldiers removed what was left of the choir, taking away the walls that had buttressed the east side of the

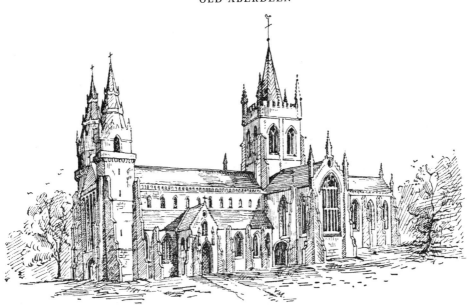

St Machar's Cathedral as it would have looked before the fall of Elphinstone's spire, centre. If the spire and central tower, the south transept below and choir, extreme right, are covered, the section on the left side is all that remains of the cathedral today.

central tower, capped since the loss of the spire by a quaint saddle-backed roof. For several years afterwards the tower had looked as though it was about to fall down, so it came as no surprise when it eventually crashed in 1688. Piles of stones were scattered about and some jagged masonry was left standing. There was no thought of rebuilding. Loose stones could be sold off as building materials, providing a welcome source of income for the impecunious parish kirk of Old Machar as the cathedral had become. Sales were advertised by William Walker drumming through the streets of Old Aberdeen to announce the latest roup of fallen masonry. In the years that followed cathedral stones were used to repair the Powis Brig, the stairs of the council chamber, 'the old work of King's College' which 'turned ruinous' with regularity. A prime batch of hewn stones was even stolen to mend the fabric of Gavin Dunbar's Hospital next door to the cathedral.

Neither transept fared well. In 1638 the north aisle (transept) was sold to the 2nd Marquis of Huntly as a family mausoleum, though he joined its clientele rather earlier than he might have expected, being beheaded in 1649. On the night of November 1719, the top of Gordon's Aisle, as it had become known, was 'thrown down by an extraordinary tempest of wind and rain', which broke the gravestone of the Marquis's kinsman, Sir Alexander Gordon of Cluny, providing more debris to sell. Six years later, according to the Old Aberdeen chronicler William Orem, 'the masters of [King's] College caused workmen to take down the top of the [south] aisle to help build anew the south side of the college'. Thus by a quirk of fate, stones from Dunbar's burial aisle were used to build the new 'piazza' range at King's College, which replaced his own south range, Dunbar's Building.

The nave, the people's part of the cathedral, built by Henry de Lichtoun in the fifteenth century, survived with Dunbar's heraldic ceiling and his twin towers still intact. Its shape and acoustics made it an ideal preaching kirk. The Kirk Session walled it up at the east end and strived to keep it wind and watertight. That is all that remains of the cathedral.

THE VIA CANONIA
*

The canons, who were responsible for running both the Cathedral and the diocese of Aberdeen, lived in the Via Canonia, the Canons' Road or Chanonry. Their manses lined the approaches to St Machar's, the 'tails' or long rigs of their gardens forming the glebes. That medieval layout remains. The manses of the treasurer, dean, precentor and chancellor of St Machar's occupied a prime position opposite the cathedral where Nos 13–16 Chanonry now stand. After the Reformation some clergy stayed on, unmolested, in their manses, some abandoned them and others sold them or passed them on to relatives.

THE MANSE OF BIRSE
*

Only the Chancellor's Manse of Birse, the most easterly of the row opposite the cathedral, survived into relatively modern times. It dated from the sixteenth century and replaced earlier buildings on the site. The chancellor was secretary of the diocese, the cathedral's lawyer and librarian. A secret passage from Birse to the cathedral kept his comings and goings private. When the clouds of the Reformation were gathering, the incumbent chancellor Alexander Seaton handed his manse over to a relative. Thereafter it had a number of eminent owners and was extended and partly rebuilt in the early eighteenth century by the Buchans of Cairnbulg. By the mid-nineteenth century it even had a street number, No. 16, the only pre-Reformation Chanonry manse to have survived long enough to acquire one.

In 1887 the owner, Miss Nicola Buchan of Auchmacoy, died and it was

The Chancellor's Manse of Birse. Demolition is about to begin.

bought by Mr Leslie of Fetternear who demolished it. Mrs Trail, chronicler of Old Aberdeen, denounced this as 'sacrilege'. In 1935 a handsome new No. 16, in red sandstone, was built on the site by the architect A. G. R. Mackenzie, incorporating in its outer wall part of the wall of the sixteenth-century manse.

GAVIN DUNBAR'S HOSPITAL
✳

In 1531, towards the end of his life, Bishop Dunbar founded an almshouse for indigent elderly men of good character at the north end of the Chanonry, immediately west of St Machar's Cathedral, beside the present Seaton Park entrance. The beadsmen (for so they were called after their custom of count-ing beads as they prayed) were granted ten merks a year and a merk to buy a white surcoat. Their day began at dawn with the chanting of prayers in the oratory on the south side of the house. The afternoon was spent working in the garden and the orchard where herbs and fruit were grown. There were more prayers before supper at six, and the outer door was closed by 8 p.m.

In the founding charter, Dunbar gave details of size, layout, rules and regulations. 'The house of the hospital shall be 100 feet long, and about 32 feet wide, and it shall be divided so as to accommodate twelve poor men in sepa-

Gavin Dunbar's Hospital, with its timber steeple, from the drawing by Andrew Gibb.

rate rooms.' Twelve reflected the number of Christ's disciples. Each room had a fireplace and there was a common-room on the north side of the house and a kitchen. Meals were to be taken 'in their own rooms or in the common room if they can manage so to agree among themselves that they can all dine at the same time'. The old men, it seems, were expected to be quarrelsome.

The hospital continued its good work after the Reformation. The active beadsmen got out and about and the Old Aberdeen records provide glimpses of their activities. Some were troublemakers. In 1609 Thomas Baverlay was fined 40 shillings 'for giffing of Janet Lamb ane cuff'. Some must have been able to read for in 1641 Master Alexander Gordon left all his books to the hospital. The glebe of Monymusk Manse next door, running down to the present Seaton Park was also gifted to the hospital, giving the old men more ground to cultivate. In May 1679 they complained to the town council that their land had been trampled and destroyed by local vandals.

In 1714, Colonel John Middleton, a Hanoverian officer and a son of

Principal George Middleton of King's College, bought the Seaton Estate and later, Dunbar's Hospital and lands, though the beadsmen remained. James Forbes of Newe, merchant and money lender, acquired Seaton in 1781 and later offered Baillie Logan's Lodging, a property in Don Street, as a home for the beadsmen in exchange for Dunbar's Hospital which he then demolished, incorporating the grounds into the Seaton estate.

SEATON HOUSE

*

At one time the address of Seaton House was given as 'The Chanonry' in the Aberdeen Post Office Directories, so it is appropriate to include it here. In 1641, James Gordon, a lawyer and a baillie of Old Aberdeen, was granted a charter by Robert Keith of Seaton of part of 'the land and the ville of Seytoun' and was also to have 'ane ferrie boat upon the watter of Don adjacent to the said lands'.

Gordon built a family home close by the river and when Colonel Middleton (who was his maternal grandson) took the reins at Seaton, he incorporated his grandfather's house as the north-west wing of a new, Georgian building which formed the south front.

Three generations of Middletons lived together at Seaton House: the Hanoverian colonel, later MP for Aberdeen Burghs; his father, Principal George Middleton, an inveterate Jacobite who was taken in by the colonel after being turned out of King's College when the Rising of 1715 collapsed;

Bailie James Gordon's original mid-seventeenth-century Seaton House.

and the colonel's son George, who became an improving laird. All three were subscribers to James Gibbs' *Book of Architecture* (1728), and the new south front of Seaton House is thought to have been inspired by some of the plates in the Gibbs' Book. It is quite likely that, Gibbs, a friend of the colonel, was the architect.

James Forbes of Newe acquired the Seaton estate from Lady Diana, George Middleton's widow, and on his death the estate passed to his daughter, Elizabeth, and her husband, Lord James Hay, an aide-de-camp of Wellington's at Waterloo. They travelled widely on the continent and brought home fine furnishings and china, even packets of seed for the garden. In time the property was inherited by their grandson, Major Malcolm Hay, a noted Catholic scholar and renowned soldier. In 1947 Seaton House and its policies, 98 acres in all, were purchased from Major Hay by Aberdeen Town Council (from the Common Good Fund) for £18,000. The house was burned down when the council were still thinking of a use for it, and it was demolished in 1963. The home estate of Seaton, formerly the Bogforth of the Bishops of Aberdeen, became Seaton Park, open to the public.

The eighteenth-century frontage of Seaton House was built of local brick, with quoins of dressed sandstone and a slated, piended roof. The pedimented main entrance had a splendid tripartite window and was originally topped by stone urns and a cupola.

THE UNIVERSITY OF ABERDEEN

As soon as the pious and astute William Elphinstone, chancellor of Scotland, was consecrated bishop of the diocese of Aberdeen in 1488, he set about realising his long-nurtured vision of creating a new university. St Andrew's and Glasgow Universities had been founded by the bishops of their respective dioceses to serve the east and west of the country. Elphinstone, a favourite mentor of the young king, James IV, now took up the cause of the north, 'in which dwell men who are rude and ignorant of letters and almost barbarous'. Northern barbarians had been making their way to the existing universities of Scotland and of Europe for some considerable time but Elphinstone was laying it on thick for the Pope, whose sanction was essential. At last, with the Foundation Bull of 10 February 1495 secure in his baggage, the bishop returned to Scotland from Rome and began the revenue chasing and the head hunting necessary to fund the building and staffing of his new university.

He decided to locate it in his personal fiefdom of Old Aberdeen where his writ ran without challenge. At that time it consisted of St Machar's

King's College, c. 1670, once attributed to George Jamesone.
Aberdeen in Byegone Days, *Robert Anderson, 1910.*

Cathedral, the ecclesiastical close of the Chanonry, plus 'three or four houses of inhabitants there'. Old Aberdeen sometimes appears in old records simply as 'The Chanonry'. On his arrival, Elphinstone defined its boundaries, pushing the limits south towards the Spital and scarcely a year after his ordination prevailed on King James to erect the marsh-ridden Old Aberdeen as a burgh of barony, a host town for the new university. This he had decided to locate at the south end, as far as he could from the cathedral's influence, yet within the burgh boundary.

KING'S COLLEGE

*

The site near the Powis Burn was particularly boggy and had to be overlaid with 'great rafters of oake', according to Parson Gordon, before building work could begin around 1497. The new university was ground-breaking in other ways. The Foundation Bull provided for the instruction of laymen in law and medicine as well as the usual teaching of philosophy and theology to aspiring clerics. And though the college was laid out in the traditional defensive style of four ranges forming a quadrangle, it was custom-built, which was an innovation in Scotland. St Andrew's and Glasgow Universities were housed in a variety of buildings in the early days while Marischal College in Aberdeen, founded nearly a hundred years after King's, had to make do, for a century and a half with those of the Greyfriars' monastic buildings which had survived the attentions of the 'rascal multitude' during the Reformation. King's College – though dedicated to the Virgin Mary, that name, in the King's honour, had quickly caught on – dominated the approach to Old Aberdeen. The traveller on his way north, passing the wee thackit cottages of the Spital, must have stopped awestruck in his tracks.

The chapel and the principal's apartment forming the north and west ranges, and the east range with the Great Hall, for dining, and the public school, for assembly, below, were up and running by 1505. No further work in the quadrangle was complete by the time Elphinstone died in 1514. The residential quarters of the south range with its flanking towers were begun but not finished. The library was not even started. The splendid crown tower, Old Aberdeen's most famous icon, could not have been complete. The five 'great bells' commissioned by Elphinstone were not cast until 1519. It comes as a shock to realise that the founder never saw the completed crown tower and that King James, slain at Flodden, was unaware of the compliment paid him in the shape of the imperial crown.

DUNBAR'S BUILDING

*

It fell to Gavin Dunbar, Bishop of Aberdeen (1517–32), to assume Elphinstone's mantle as Chancellor of the fledgling university. He oversaw the completion of the residential quarters, Dunbar's Building, which was occupied by the undergraduates for whom living-in was compulsory, and by their masters. The fourteen chambers and the two flanking towers, named after the signs of the zodiac, were simply furnished with beds, usually two to a chamber, little tables and benches of oak or fir. Of the two towers, Jove to the west was part of the residential range, while the easterly tower, Scorpio, was the first of the college's several libraries, later becoming a sort of glory hole as well as housing the college's ramshackle armoury.

After Dunbar's death the library was built, at last, by Bishop William Stewart, chancellor of King's from 1532–45. It was a lean-to building set against the chapel, as planned by Elphinstone. The ground floor contained the college strongroom and a classroom. The library was on the upper floor, linked by a little door to the rood loft of the chapel.

THE NEW WORK
AND THE TIMBER MUSES

*

The years following the Reformation, and the Covenanting era, were catastrophic for the college and its fabric. Buildings fell into decay and the masters who were responsible for their maintenance were sometimes indolent, sometimes preoccupied with affairs of state and often, disastrously for the management of the college, against the government of the day. It fell to the more committed and forceful of the principals and chancellors to organise the patching up of the fabric and most importantly, the seeking out of benefactors.

With student numbers increasing, additional halls of residence were required and it was found easier to build new ones than to tackle Dunbar's Building, which was said now to be 'much dilapidated' and beyond repair. The New Work or Square Work, a 'tower block', was initiated during the principalship of Dr William Guild, none other, and from 1582 developed by Principal John Row, a noted Hebrew scholar. It was built in a 'gap site' in the north-east corner of the quad and originally contained twenty-four rooms on six floors, accommodating numerous students. It is noted here under false pretences, for it still exists as the Cromwell Tower, though its annex does not.

This vignette from Parson Gordon's Plan is the earliest drawing of the quadrangle of King's College. Moving counter-clockwise from the chapel and crown tower, the building fronting College Bounds contained the principal's apartments. The tower, Jove, left and Dunbar's Building dominate the foreground. The corbie-stepped gable-end, right, belonged to the Great Hall. The right-hand tower, Scorpio, is now the Round Tower. The Great Hall ran between Scorpio and the New Work (later the Cromwell Tower), with its roof not yet completed. Wedged between the New Work and the east end of the chapel is the tiny Timber Muses. Bishop Stewart's Library is the low lean-to building against the chapel.

This was the Timber Muses, a muse being a study, a three-storey wooden residence with a bell tower. It was wedged between the east end of the chapel and the New Work and was removed when a stair wing was added to the latter during one of its many 'makeovers' down the centuries.

FRASER'S BUILDINGS
✳

Bishop Stewart's lean-to library began to leak where the roof met the chapel wall and it had to be largely rebuilt in 1617. Later, as the result of an Act of Parliament of 1709, there were too many books. King's College was one of the four Scottish universities entitled to receive a copy of all books published by Stationers' Hall in London, which at that time enjoyed the monopoly on publishing. By 1719 books were lying everywhere; the shelves were full and there was nowhere to put them. A few years later the roof fell in, again. Fortunately one of the masters had made the acquaintance of James Fraser, thanks to whose generosity the old library was taken down and a new building erected on the same site against the chapel, with classrooms on the ground floor and a new library above, nearly double the length of the old one. Fraser also gifted his own library. He was a King's graduate hailing from Inverness, an excellent scholar who went to London to 'push his fortune'. He became tutor to young noblemen including the Duke of St Albans, the son of Charles II and Nell Gwyn. When the king founded the Royal Hospital, Chelsea, for Army veterans (hence Chelsea Pensioners) in 1690, he appointed Fraser as its first secretary. Fraser held office through the next four reigns. He was careful with his money and put it to good use during his retirement.

Fraser was also prevailed on to fund a new residential range on the site of Dunbar's Building. Completed by 1730, it was built from the Dunbar downtakings and stones from the south transept at St Machar's Cathedral which had fallen in. It was a higher building than its predecessor and the ground floor was fronted by a neo-classical piazza, a square-columned arcade. Before the days of students' unions and coffee bars, undergraduates could meet here and shelter from the rain and cold between lectures.

The north side of Fraser's 'piazza' building with the arcaded ground floor is to the right. The Great Hall building is centre. The New Work (Cromwell Tower), the roof now completed, is left.

It ceased to be compulsory for students to reside at the university after 1775. Fraser's building had come rather late on the scene as a hall of residence, but it lingered on for years. Describing it in the 1850s in *Life at a Northern University*, Neil Maclean wrote:

> The rooms are still to be seen if you take the trouble to walk up the stair that leads past the Moral Philosophy classroom, deserted and bare, but still retaining many a mark of those who once lived and wrought there.

The Frontage and the South Range
*

The principal's residence, dating back to Elphinstone's time, was removed some time after 1773 and various designs were put forward for an elegant, fashionable frontage to the college, including one by a 'Mr Adam', though which one is uncertain. Another design, by the Jacobite, James Byres of Tonley, involved enveloping the front of the college within a neo-classical palazzo. These proved too expensive or too outré and eventually the Aberdeen city architect, John Smith, provided the present façade, in Abbotsford Gothic which blends with the chapel. Some people are never satisfied and it was much criticised at the time.

Fusion with Marischal College was imminent by the late 1850s. New lecture rooms were essential to cope with the influx from Broad Street but fortunately Government finance was now available. Fraser's 'piazza' Building was demolished in 1860, and replaced by the extant range of lecture rooms. The tower Jove survived for a time as a stump. At this time the south side of the quadrangle was pushed back about five metres (the join shows), and somehow reorganised to leave the Round Tower, formerly the Ivy and originally Scorpio, outside, where it remains, its gunloop intact. It would have been demolished had it not been for the intervention of the historian Dr John Hill Burton.

The Chapel Library
*

There is a story that Fraser's library, tucked in below the chapel, was burned down in a mysterious fire, but the truth of the matter seems that it was in as

King's College after 1773, minus a frontage. The library had moved into the chapel and the principal's residence had been demolished. There is a good view of the Cromwell Tower and its turret. The tiny turret of the Timber Muses, scarcely visible, is in front of it, and to its right, the Great Hall. The building appearing on the right is No. 52 College Bounds, built from the down-takings of the lean-to chapel library.

bad a way as its predecessor, when it was pulled down as part of a building scheme in 1773. The downtakings were used to build the two manses for the professors of Mathematics and Greek. As Nos 50 and 52 College Bounds, they were used as such well into the twentieth century and are now student offices. What happened to all the books? The nave or ante-chapel at the west end of the chapel, then 'neglected and disused' was fitted up as the college library.

Visitors found the chapel-turned-library most intriguing. Francis Douglas in his *Description of the East Coast of Scotland*, 1782 wrote:

> A noble room ... nearly one half of the chapel. In the west end is a high Gothic window and from the centre of the wall below begins a screw stair spreading to both sides of the room and leading to galleries which occupy the whole length. The books which are very numerous, and many of them curious, are arranged in excellent order.

Judging by past performance things could only deteriorate. Around 1850 the artist R. W. Billings noted that the library roof, part of the original chapel roof, was suffering from damp, and the books 'including some fine specimens

of medieval art exposed to great danger'. By the time of Billings' visit, the chapel library was also beginning to run out of space and as fusion with Marischal loomed a custom-built library to serve not only King's College but a united university was a priority. Where should the new library go? The medieval Great Hall over on the east range was still extant, but only just. The beautiful ceiling, deemed past repair, had been smashed up early in the nineteenth century. The whole building now went. 'The mid-Victorians fell upon it in 1860 and ruthlessly destroyed it,' wrote the university librarian P. J. Anderson. Its loss was much regretted. However the east range was just the place for the next library building, and those books which had survived ordeal by water, if not, perhaps by fire, went on another short journey round the quad. Here King's College Library, familiar to so many graduates, was built. This library was extended eastwards in 1884, ran out of space a century later and became a conference centre in 1991.

Above. The former King's College Library. It was the chapel library writ large. The architect, Robert Matheson of the Office of Works, had striven to reproduce the chapel's ceiling, stairs, west window and galleries. Tables and chairs were not introduced until the 1930s. The stained glass of the great window was blown out when a bomb landed nearby during the war. The replacement windows are less ornate.

Left. The nave of King's College Chapel as library. By R. W. Billings.

THE
DIVINITY MANSE
*

Robert Matheson's brief covered the provision of college manses as well as new teaching accommodation and as a result the amazing Divinity (or Theology) manse in French Gothic style made its appearance in 1867, probably the work of Matheson's assistant Hippolyte Jean Blanc. It sat north of the chapel on the original burial grounds of King's College, on the lawn where students now relax in summer.

The next expansion, New King's, was to be a new open quadrangle, with the chapel as its south range, the north range consisting of lecture rooms on the site of the Old Aberdeen brewery, the west range open to the north end of College Bounds. These were completed by 1912 with A. Marshall Mackenzie as architect. The First World War halted building for several years but in 1926 Marshall Mackenzie & Son began work on the Elphinstone Hall which would form the east range of the new quadrangle. This new Hall was staked out on the herbaceous border of Divinity Manse. Squeezed out after an existence of scarcely fifty years, the Manse was duly demolished and re-erected, much truncated, across the road in open land which in 1963

Divinity Manse, left, sits at right angles to King's College Chapel.

became Johnston Hall of Residence. Divinity Manse had been given its marching orders but whither?

The surviving early buildings of the King's College quadrangle are the chapel (1500), its Crown Tower (*c.* 1520), and the Cromwell Tower (from 1582). The Round Tower, old Scorpio (*c.* 1525), is out at the back.

THE COLLEGE BOUNDS: THE UNIVERSITY MANSES

*

Bishop Elphinstone planned his university very carefully. While the young students studied ate and slept within the quadrangle of King's College, the area immediately outside the college was laid out as an extra-mural campus. Here Elphinstone built manses (residences) for his senior members of staff, and for the humanist who taught Latin or Humanity as it was then called. The manses were according to Orem 'furnished as if they had been so many little colleges', which is what they were. The whole area formed the 'colledge boundis' of which King's College was the focal point. Parson Gordon's Plan of 1661 illustrates it a century and more after its heyday.

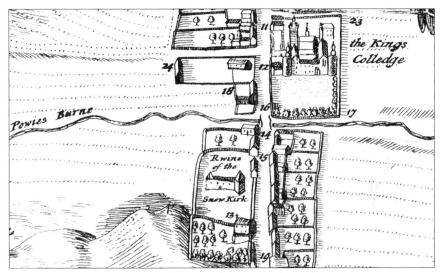

No. 13, left, is the humanist's two-storey manse in its well-stocked glebe.
Beyond is the Snow Kirk. No. 14 is the Powis Brig with the Powis Burn flowing under-
neath. Beyond is the college garden, right, and a miniature sketch of King's College.
No. 18, opposite, marks 'the Twelve Roods', Professor Alexander Fraser's Powis
estate at an early stage of its development. Left of No. 12 is the manse of the
mediciner. From Gordon's Plan of 1661.

COLLEGE BOUNDS

THE SNOW KIRK
*

St Mary of the Snows was the parish church of Old Aberdeen, built by Bishop Elphinstone who was a devotee of the cult of St Maria Maggiore ad Nives in Rome, Great St Mary of the Snows. St Mary's Old Aberdeen was not great, but a plain kirk, deliberately so, one suspects, in order not to detract from King's College Chapel on the other side of the highway. It was known as the Snow or Snaw Kirk, usually just the Snaw.

In 1583 James VI instructed the Snaw congregation to worship at St Machar's while the revenues of the Snaw, were granted to King's College whose masters were ordered to 'demoleishe and tak doun the ruinous walls and tymber of Snaw' to repair St Machar's'. Commendable though King James' sense of economy was, there was an ulterior motive. He complained that the kirks were 'abusit to superstition and idolatrie', i.e. banned practices such as saying mass. But Old Aberdeen folk looked on the Snaw as their true

Slezer's 'Old Aberdeen' is dominated on the right by the Snaw Kirk. It had a corbie-stepped gable and a simple belfry which housed two bells, ex-St Machar's, the gift of Bishop Elphinstone. They were called Schohtmadony (shuggle Madonna) and Skellat (Scots for a small bell). The dark building, centre, opposite King's College, is the mediciner's manse. St Machar's Cathedral sports its saddleback roof above the central tower. Theatrum Scotiae, John Slezer, 1688.

parish church. Secret burials took place there, combining the comfort of burial in a familiar place with avoidance of interment dues charged at St Machar's. Hidden from prying eyes the Snaw was a favourite spot where 'men and boyes usually playit kits [quoits] in time of sermon' much to the annoyance of the Cathedral's enforcement officers.

The Royal injunction of 1583 to demolish the Snaw was not fully carried out. After Dr William Guild became Principal of King's College in 1640, as well as taking down the Bishop's Palace, he 'yokit George Ronald, mason, to the Snaw Kirk, and cast down the walls thereof, such as was standing and caused transport the stones to big up the College yard dykes ... whereat many Oldtown people murmured'.

By 1671 burials at the Snaw were legitimised. If people were going to be buried there willy nilly, the masters of King's decided they might as well charge interment fees, gaining welcome revenue for the college. Burials in the cemetery outside the kirk were charged at 'ane dolllar' (£12 13s 4d Scots) and in the body of the ruinous kirk 'aucht poundis Scots money'. Kirk and cemetery have long since vanished. The cemetery was under crop by the early nineteenth century and is built over, while the site of the kirk itself, located behind No. 21–31 College Bounds, now forms a graveyard for those of the Catholic faith.

THE HERMITAGE

*

Neither ecclesiastical nor academic, the Hermitage was, in its heyday, a fashionable and exotic addition to College Bounds. No. 18 on Parson Gordon's Plan, page 237, indicated the boggy 'Twelve Roods' opposite the college, bought in 1691 by the entrepreneurial Alexander Fraser, subprincipal and Professor of Greek. It was not only handy for his work; he decided to develop it as a commercial venture. 'He hath drained the mire and built two great houses and three lesser houses towards the street', wrote Orem. So began the development of the Powis estate which in time passed to his descendants, the Leslies. In 1781 Hugh Leslie had a 'House on the Hill' as it is called in the plans, built in brick on the Firhill within the now much-extended Powis grounds. The architect, George Jaffray, was an Old Aberdeen man who later designed the mansion house of Powis. The Hermitage, a retreat rather than a hermit's dwelling, was an octagonal observatory-cum-summerhouse with a secret underground chamber and an attic. It cost £149.8s 1d. These 'fun' buildings were fashionable at this time and there were several in Aberdeen. The viewing platform around the top would have allowed one to see what was going on in the quadrangle of King's College. The main rooms had plaster-work with a shell design where fashionable parties with music and card games, and suppers of oysters and porter, almonds and oranges were held. By the late nineteenth century the Firhill was known locally as the Miser's Hilly for the Hermitage was popularly believed to be the haunt of a miser (or a hermit). A ballad written around 1860 by David Grant about the mythical hermit became an instant success.

With the passing years the Hermitage was neglected and vandalised. It was demolished in 1925 and the hill sold as a sandpit. After the sand had been commercially exploited, the Firhill, now a dip rather than a hill, became the HQ and parade ground for the University's Officers' Training Corps and Air Squadron. In the 1950s one would find these wartimes colleagues Professors R. V. Jones and Edward Wright yarning at the bar of the Air Squadron mess. The area subsequently became a car park, and latterly, a central heating station.

The Hermitage in the 1920s, prior to demolition. The top of the building including the platform has been replaced by a thatched roof with a louvre on top, surmounted by an ornamental crescent matching those of the Paris Gate towers.